¡MOLAS!

¡MOLAS!

PATTERNS ■ TECHNIQUES ■ PROJECTS
FOR COLORFUL APPLIQUÉ

KATE MATHEWS

LARK BOOKS

Art Director: Dana Irwin

Photography: Evan Bracken, unless otherwise identified

Illustrations: Bernadette Wolf

Production: Bobby Gold, Dana Irwin

Library of Congress Cataloging in Publication Data

Mathews, Kate.
   Molas! : patterns, techniques, and projects for colorful appliqué
/ Kate Mathews. — 1st ed.
      p.   cm.
   Includes index.
   ISBN 1-57990-020-8
   1. Appliqué—Patterns. 2. Molas   I. Title.
TT779.M29 1998
746.44'5—dc21   97-31249
                                            CIP

10 9 8 7 6 5 4 3 2

Published by Lark Books

50 College St.

Asheville, NC 28801, US

© 1998, Lark Books

For information about distribution in the U.S., Canada, the U.K., Europe, and Asia, call Lark Books
at 828-253-0467.

Distributed in Australia by Capricorn Link (Australia) Pty Ltd., P.O. Box 6651, Baulkham Hills
Business Centre, NSW 2153, Australia

Distributed in New Zealand by Southern Publishers Group, 22 Burleigh St., Grafton, Auckland, NZ

Printed in Hong Kong by Oceanic Graphic Printing Productions Ltd.

ISBN 1-57990-020-8

CONTENTS

INTRODUCTION

Molas are the brightly colored appliqué panels made only in the San Blas region of Panama by the Kuna Indians. Despite their limited provenance, these dazzling textiles have interested collectors and inspired artists all over the world. At first sight, people who have never before seen a mola feel that they have made an exciting new discovery. They are immediately attracted by the engaging designs, brilliant hues, and meticulous stitching. After this first encounter, nearly all lovers of textiles become

appreciative collectors of the appliqué panels and they may even incorporate molas into their own art work or simply enjoy them as is, hanging on a wall or draped over the back of a chair.

This book salutes the traditionally-made molas from Panama, as well as new interpretations of this appliqué technique by contemporary artists. The Kuna women observe the world around them and stitch what they see into stunning appliqué designs—from natural flora and fauna to manmade products of the modern age. Other contemporary artists of all persuasions observe molas and then adapt or interpret mola design or technique in their own ways, from paper collage and stencil patterns to wearable art and home decorating items.

These traditional molas and contemporary interpretations are showcased in the Gallery sections of this book. Then, a diversity of how-to projects will introduce you to the step-by-step methods of making your own mola-inspired work of art. Whether you practice the traditionally stitched appliqué techniques that the Kuna women use or experiment with methods that employ modern convenience materials, you will create your own unique versions of this splendid native art form.

Mother's Day mola, from the collection of Patti Glazer.

Opposite: Geometric mola, made especially for this book by Elena Pérez.

About the Kuna Indians

LEFT: **Mola Producers Cooperative member sewing on Carti Suitupo Island.**
PHOTO: **Annie Laurie Cisneros.**

RIGHT: **A display of molas.**
PHOTO: **W.M. Christenson.**

The Kuna (also spelled Cuna) Indians live on 50 or so of the more than 365 San Blas islands off the east coast of Panama. Some also live on a narrow mainland strip and in small towns across the South American border in Colombia. These combined mainland and island areas of Panama comprise the Comarca de Kuna Yala, or Kuna territory, and this is where the world's molas are made.

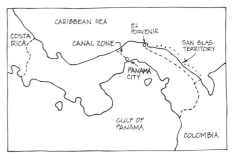

One of the inhabited San Blas Islands.
PHOTO: **Raul Cisneros.**

A BRIEF HISTORY

The Kunas have resided in the Panama/Colombia area for centuries, but did not migrate to the islands until the mid-19th century. Some anthropologists theorize that they are descendants of the coastal South American Carib tribes, adapting tribal body painting to needle and thread over time. Others suggest that they descended from Southeast Asians who traveled across the North American land bridge and migrated through the American Southwest to Central America. This theory might explain various similarities among the cultures. For example, the Kuna's mahogany dugout canoe is called "ulu," which is the same word as the curved-blade Eskimo knife. Additionally, mola design motifs are reminiscent of Hawaiian quilt patterns, Southwest Indian pottery designs, and the quilts of historic India, which are today's collectibles in Pakistan. The parallels between molas and the Hmong embroideries of Thailand are especially notable, as can be seen on page 24.

Spanish explorers encountered the Kunas in the 15th and 16th centuries. The Spaniards' systematic enslavement and slaughter of the indigenous peoples, along with the plague of European diseases they brought with them, decimated native populations. However, Kunas managed to survive successive waves of European exploration and settlement, and they traded actively with Scottish, French, and other Western European citizens during the 17th and 18th centuries. In fact, during the mid-1700s, intermarriage between the Kunas and French settlers was not uncommon.

By the mid-1800s, the Indians began migrating eastward across the Panamanian main-

> **Kunas managed to survive successive waves of European exploration and settlement.**

land to the Caribbean coast and San Blas islands about 12 miles offshore. This relocation was propelled by inland jungle disease, weather calamities, and the Indians' desire to be closer to the coastal mouths of fresh-water rivers. Also, the new island locations gave them easier access to the ships of their trading partners. The commercial activity of this period introduced cloth, scissors, needles, and thread to the Kuna, stimulating the development of needleworked clothing

Mola Producers Cooperative members sewing on Carti Suitupo Island. PHOTO: Annie Laurie Cisneros.

While molas are always hand-stitched, a sewing machine (available at the Cooperative shop) is often used to assemble the parts of a mola blouse. PHOTO: W.M. Christenson.

and body adornment. The first recorded mola-like clothing appeared in the late-1800s. While many people believe that molas are ancient forms of Kuna costume and expression, they have been made for only a little more than 100 years.

THE MODERN ERA

In 1903, Panama declared its independence from Colombia and established itself as a new country. In its programs to assert a national identity, the new Panamanian government attempted to force Kuna assimilation by banning traditional dress and religious customs. These programs were fiercely resisted for years, in an ongoing Kuna effort to create a separate nation, and periodic skirmishes throughout the early 1900s resulted in the deaths of minor Panamanian government officials and overseers.

In 1925, the Porvenir Treaty between the national government and the Kunas was signed. The treaty granted the Indians relative autonomy and a measure of self-determination regarding their own affairs. Today, a gov-

Despite continuing and increasing exposure to the outside world, they hold fast to traditional ways and work hard to defy Westernization.

ernment representative sits in the Provincial Government Office in El Porvenir and acts as liaison with the national center and overseer of Kuna self-governing bodies. While the Kunas still struggle for complete self-determination, they largely control their own local affairs and insist on active involvement in any national issues in their territory.

The seat of decision-making in each Kuna village is the *congreso*, or village meeting. Elected island leaders meet daily to discuss events and solve local problems. Because the Kuna language is unwritten, the congreso also functions as an important method of upholding oral traditions through ritual chanting and storytelling.

KUNA LIFE TODAY

The Kuna Indians lead a tribal life guided by strong traditions. Despite continuing and increasing exposure to the outside world, they hold fast to traditional ways and work hard to defy Westernization. Family incomes are derived mostly from fishing, farming coconuts for export, and sales of molas to tourists. The Kunas maintain their crops on the uninhabited San Blas islands, and sell their molas through the local chapters of the Mola Cooperative or directly to tourists when cruise ships anchor offshore.

The traditional costume

It is believed that the Kunas practiced decorative body painting until the 18th century, when French settlers introduced clothing, and body adornment was translated into painted designs on clothing. Stitched versions of the painted designs appeared late in the 19th

Kuna woman in traditional dress.
PHOTO:
W.M. Christenson.

century. Regardless of its origins, the Kuna Indian woman's traditional costume is colorful, unique, and exciting to behold. It is also a wearer's expression of pride in her Kuna identity. Essentially unchanged for the past 100 years, the woman's traditional costume consists of:

■ blouse made from two similar, but not identical, mola panels;
■ wrap or sarong skirt, called *saburet* or *saborete*, typically of blue printed cotton;

This mola, from the collection of the author, was started with three layers of fabric: black on the bottom, orange in the middle, and dark red on the top. Some of the black and orange lines are created by cutting through the top layers in reverse appliqué, but most of the black shapes are applied on top of the red layer, in overlay appliqué. The other colors are either added on top of the other layers or slipped in between the top and middle layers. The embroidery stitches contribute even more color and detail to the final design.

For extra color without wasting fabric, the Kuna women employ inlay appliqué, in which small patches of colored fabric are slipped between the top (red) layer and middle (orange) layer. The red is cut through, the edges turned under and stitched down, to reveal the inlay patch. Here, you can see the small patch of green fabric inlaid between the red and orange layers.

- cotton underskirt, called *picha*;
- head scarf, called *muswe*, typically of red and yellow printed cotton;
- trade beads, called *wini*, wrapped around legs and forearms in geometric designs;
- gold nose ring, earrings, and necklace with coins.

Kuna women also sport thong sandals, smoke pipes, and paint a dark line down their noses. Men wear a more conservative and Western outfit of white shirt and dark trousers.

While their clothing is unique to Kuna culture, its components are surprisingly international. For example, the mola panels are crafted of fabrics imported from Colombia and China. The red and yellow head scarves are lengths of cotton from Japan, preprinted in repeating squares. The necklace coins are from Panama, Colombia, and the United States. And the wini, or trade beads, are from Czechoslovakia. The beads are strung in a single strand, following a pre-planned threading arrangement so they form a geometric design when wound around the leg or forearm.

THE MOLA

The word mola can mean "cloth," "clothing," or "blouse," although it has come to signify to most people the stitched panel itself. Almost all Kuna women make molas, not as a pastime but as an important source of family revenue. Women sew as much as possible and wherever they may be—during meetings, between household chores, and while visiting or waiting for transportation. Girls learn to make molas at a very young age, as early as four or five years old, and by the time they are seven or eight, they are helping their elders by stitching backgrounds and completing other simple details. By the time they marry, most young women have become quite skillful stitchers and have completed many mola blouses.

▮▮▮ A woman might spend up to a total of 100 hours completing a mola.

Until tourism exploded in the region in the 1960s and sales to visitors became commonplace, molas were almost all sewn exclusively for the maker's own use and wear. A woman might spend up to a total of 100 hours completing a mola, in time periods spread out over four to six weeks. Because a well-made mola is a

ABOVE RIGHT: **The black birds and the turquoise and other outlines around the birds are applied on top of the mola layers, in overlay appliqué. Then, chain stitch embroidery with one strand of thread and running stitches with two strands of thread add fine detail to the design shapes after they are appliquéd in position.**

RIGHT: **On the back side of this mola, you can see that the tiny hand stitches are made through all the fabric layers and neatly tied off.**

PHOTOS:
W.M. Christenson.

source of pride, its maker takes great care in planning the design, cutting the pattern precisely, and stitching the layers invisibly. Despite their quality construction, molas don't survive long because of the hot and humid climate and repeated washings. The oldest mola on record was collected in 1909 and is now at the Smithsonian Institution in Washington, D.C.

The mola blouse

Mola panels were traditionally made for the backs and fronts of women's blouses. Today, molas are sold by themselves, as decorative items, or they may be made into miniature versions, called molitas, and incorporated into tote bags, eyeglass cases, and other gift items.

For the traditional blouse, panels of cotton yardage are cut or torn to the dimensions of the wearer and then layered, cut, and stitched by hand in various appliqué techniques to form the mola design (see page 36 for more about the appliqué construction techniques). The front and back panels of the blouse are usually very similar, but not quite identical, and the pieces cut from one may be used to form the design in the other (see page 45 for more information on

this waste-no-fabric method of sewing). Once the main design is completed, plain areas of the background are also worked. It is rare to find a mola with large areas of uncut or unstitched material. Finally, embroidery may be added for decorative effect or to emphasize design details.

When the mola panels are finished, they are assembled into the blouse. The molas themselves are always stitched by hand, but a sewing machine available at the Cooperative may be used to construct the finished garment. The blouse fabric is a lightweight cotton print, quite a contrast to the hefty, layered mola panel. First, the front and back molas are attached to the yoke and hemline border or ruffle. Then, puffed sleeves are attached, the neckline is edged and gathered, and a drawstring is inserted. Decorative braid or rickrack may be added to hide seams or for a decorative finish. In most molas made for sale, rickrack has replaced the time-consuming hand-stitched sawtooth edge, but you will still occasionally see the sawtooth design, called *dientes*, made by the most expert stitchers.

Sources of design inspiration

The Kuna women look to their own lives and the world around them for design ideas. Geometric

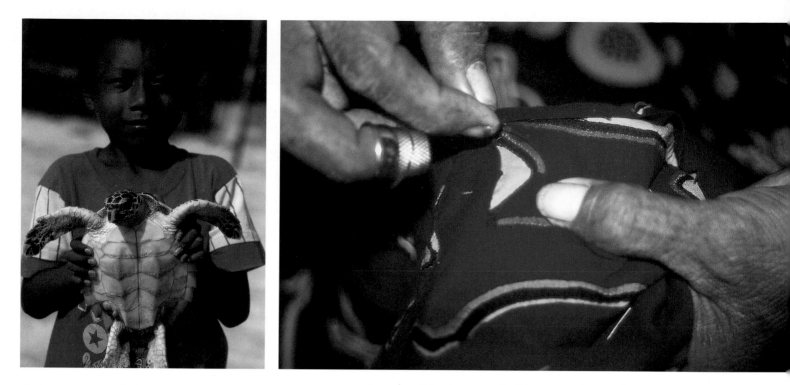

designs, mazes, and abstract patterns are common choices, but anything a woman notices during a regular day might find its way into a mola. And as her experience of the outside world has expanded, so has the variety and diversity of the motifs she may stitch.

Design sources from the natural world include native animals (iguanas, lizards, parrots, fish), local vegetation (palm trees, coconut crops, sea grasses), and the shapes of the coral reefs around the San Blas islands. Animals from other parts of the world or from books, posters, and the Bible, such as elephants, horses, and the great whale, Moby Dick, also appear in molas.

Village life and tribal religion are rich sources of design ideas. Images can include coconut farming, fishing, daily congreso meetings, mola-making, cooking, sporting events, and religious ceremonials. Because of their island location, the Kunas are regular users of transportation to their crops, fresh water sources, and mainland destinations. Molas might depict dugout canoes, Colombian commercial vessels, cruise ships, airplanes, helicopters, and even a spaceship.

Other ideas have come from Christian imagery, construction of the Panama Canal, political posters,

movies, advertising images, television, magazines and newspapers, and all manner of product packaging. It may be surprising, but not unusual, to encounter a brand-name cola bottle, cigarette pack, or industry trademark stitched into a mola. Even the cruise ships and tourists are fair game for women seeking ideas for their next mola.

Some molas have letters and words in them, especially if the design was taken from a printed source. However, because the native Kuna language is unwritten, letter forms and words have no literal meaning. Therefore, they are seen simply as design forms and may be redrawn, altered, or stitched in unusual arrangements—upside down, backwards, merged with other letters. A political slogan taken from a poster or a product name from a can label may very well appear in a mola with a backward "E" or differently curved "S."

The array of mola designs is impressive and every one is as unique as its maker. When faced with an assortment to choose from, most mola enthusiasts and collectors will be pained to narrow it down to a special one. Each mola is different, and every one is bound to have intriguing designs, colors, and details that make it truly hard to resist, in favor of another one.

ABOVE RIGHT: **Mola Producers Cooperative member sewing on Carti Suitupo Island.** PHOTO: **Raul Cisneros.**

ABOVE LEFT: **Turtles and other native animals may inspire mola designs.** PHOTO: **W.M. Christenson.**

Cooperative members of the Carti Suitupo Chapter. PHOTO: **Annie Laurie Cisneros**

THE MOLA COOPERATIVE

In 1967, an American Peace Corps project worked with Kuna women to market hand-sewn items as an income source. The children's clothes, headbands, eyeglass cases, neckties, and other items were all decorated with molas. However, the project wasn't terribly successful because the Peace Corps members recommended the use of sewing machines for production

INSET, BELOW: **Mola Producers Cooperative office in Panama City.** PHOTO: **Raul Cisneros.**

San Blas island with traditional houses and coconut palms. PHOTO: **W.M. Christenson.**

and the Kuna women didn't share the value of machine-made goods.

Based on input from Kuna women, the project shifted its focus to concentrate on marketing the molas themselves, to increase revenue, and to organize the

mola-makers. A cooperative, called Los Productores de Molas R.L., was set up in Panama City to sell molas and other handmade items from all over the country. It was also a center for education, member services, and economic development. After the Peace Corps left Panama, co-op activities and membership declined sharply, but several committed women kept the idea alive and worked to keep the project active.

Today, the Cooperative has nearly 1500 members in 14 local chapters throughout the San Blas region. Its goal is to create a steady national and international market for the sale of molas and to support Co-op members through collective purchasing of raw materials, access to loans, education, and political advocacy.

Prior to the organization of the Cooperative, mola-makers received token payments for their products, but today members receive most of the sale price of the molas they make. Membership is passed on from mother to daughter, and many local chapters have built their own co-op buildings to serve as meeting place and sales outlet. Through the Cooperative, Kuna women have become adept business managers and politically active in the economic development of the San Blas region. As a result, molas have become one of the most important products of the Kuna economy.

Gallery of Traditional Molas

In this gallery of molas, you can see the traditional Kuna appliqué techniques—reverse appliqué, overlay appliqué, and inlay appliqué. The variety of design themes illustrates that the Kuna women can translate just about anything they see in the world around them into a mola. From geometrics and mazes to animal and plant forms, the subjects of molas are as individual as the women who make them. Similarities of design and technique among appliqué textiles from other countries are strikingly apparent in the examples on pages 24-25. These resemblances may prove the anthropologists to be correct when they theorize that the Kuna Indians and Southeast Asians may have the same ancestors.

Windmill, from the collection of Charlotte Patera. One can only guess what activities are going on around the windmill.
PHOTO: **Charlotte Patera.**

ABOVE: Geometric mola, made especially for the cover of this book by Eloira Pérez

ABOVE RIGHT: Flora and fauna mola, from the collection of Rob Pulleyn.

**Eagle with alligator, from the collection of Charlotte Patera. This mola was made by an expert stitcher, as can be seen in the even edges and smooth lines.
PHOTO: Charlotte Patera.**

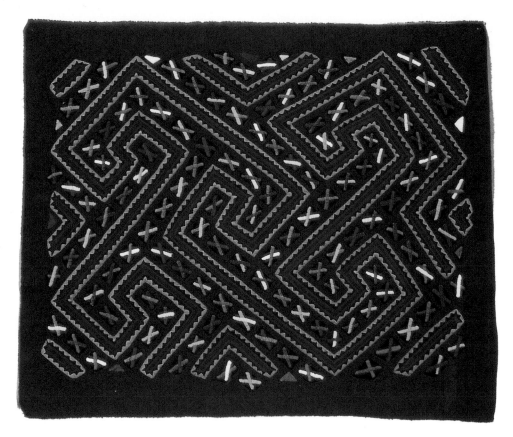

Meandering trail with sawtooth edge, from the collection of **Charlotte Patera**. PHOTO: **Charlotte Patera**.

Bird in a tree mola pillow, from the collection of **Patti Glazer**.

Four crabs, from the collection of **Charlotte Patera**.
Crab and lobster provide a source of income to the Kuna Indians.
PHOTO: **Charlotte Patera**.

Three flowers, from the collection of Charlotte Patera. Tiny black overlay squares are stitched to the yellow flower outlines. PHOTO: Charlotte Patera.

Parrot mola, made especially for this book by Trinidad Martinez

Mola blouse, part of the Kuna woman's traditional costume. The front and back are made from similar hand-stitched molas, which are then attached to the yoke, sleeves, and hem ruffle.

Leafy branches, from the collection of Charlotte Patera. Tiny embroidery stitches form the veins in the leaves.
PHOTO: **Charlotte Patera.**

Geometric molas, from the collection of Rob Pulleyn.

Old two-color mola, from the collection of Dana Irwin. This mola probably dates from the 1940s or 1950s, since the use of multi-colored designs was not widespread until tourism accelerated in the 1960s.

ABOVE: **A special X-pattern mola designed and duplicated on the island of Achutupo for a special celebration, from the collection of Charlotte Patera. PHOTO: Charlotte Patera.**

ABOVE LEFT: **Concentric zigzags, from the collection of Charlotte Patera. PHOTO: Charlotte Patera.**

LEFT: **Scorpion, from the collection of Charlotte Patera. This mola shows how the Kuna women can embellish the creatures in their everyday environment. PHOTO: Charlotte Patera.**

Appliqué Around the World

Antique appliqué quilt top from historic India (now Pakistan), from the collection of Dana Irwin. The similarity between the design motifs of this quilt top and the molas from Panama is notable.

Hmong appliquéd and embroidered panels look very similar to molas, suggesting that the Hmong people of Southeast Asia and the Kuna Indians of Panama may be descended from the same Asian ancestors.

Large Hmong appliquéd and embroidered panel, from the collection of Dana Irwin.

Small Hmong appliquéd and embroidered panels, from the collection of the author.

Zomba Designs is based in the Zomba Mountains of Southern Malawi, a little known and very rural country in East Africa, bordered by Mozambique and Tanzania. Most Malawians live in traditional villages where poverty is high, literacy is low, and daily life is a step back in time. Each day, women make the trek to village bore holes, carrying the family water supply in big pots balanced on their heads. The cash for soap, paraffin, matches, sugar, salt, and other basic necessities is earned through temporary day labor, wherever it can be found.

Tourism had been actively discouraged in the years before I arrived in 1993, with an international development project, and those who visited found few locally-made items for sale. Traditional woodcarving, pottery, and canework survived, but handmade needlework was nonexistent in local markets, in spite of the fact that many women are highly skilled in sewing for their own homes.

Zomba Designs was organized to provide income-generating opportunities for the local women. Inspired by the molas from Panama, Islamic prayer rugs from Egypt, banners and dance costumes from West Africa, Hmong textiles, and appliqué quilts from India and Pakistan, I worked with the group to develop designs for their hand-appliquéd projects. Because most village women have heavy household and family responsibilities, sewing time is limited. Members do most of the sewing in their own homes and meet weekly to turn in finished work for sale, try out new ideas, and critique fellow members' work.

The most colorful and durable local fabric is the cotton manufactured for school uniforms. It comes in about fourteen colors and this is what the women who have joined Zomba Designs use to make pillow covers, bags, quilts, and wall hangings. Most of the items are sold locally, but opportunities for international marketing are slowly developing.

—*Pamela Brooke, a Washington, D.C. writer/designer currently living and working in Malawi.*

ABOVE RIGHT: **Mayi Singano, one of the members of Zomba Designs in Malawi, East Africa, with her appliquéd wallhangings and pillows.**
PHOTOS: **Pamela Brooke.**

Gallery of Mola-Inspired Works

Artists around the world have been influenced by mola design and technique, as you can see in this gallery of contemporary works. The traditional layering of colors and fabrics has been combined with modern convenience materials to produce entirely new expressions of color and creativity. Traditional molas from Panama will surely continue to inspire artists of all persuasions.

Jenni Bateman,
Bezalel & Oholiab.
Appliquéd fabric.

"Bezalel and Oholiab were the men God appointed as the chief artisans and teachers to design and decorate the Tabernacle."

Dewey Lee Cornay,
Mola Jambalaya.
San Blas mola,
Guatemalan cot-
tons, ethnic batik
fabrics, braid,
beads; 3rd Place
winner in the 1997
American Quilter's
Society Show.

RIGHT:
Lynn Sward, *Mixed Media Mola Pins.* Polymer clay, gift wrapping paper, metallic powders, permanent marking pens.

FAR RIGHT:
Catherine Reurs, *Needlepoint Mola Slippers.*

Nancy Prichard, *School Daze.* Dyed handmade paper collage.

Gail Ferrick, *Balboa High School '64—Go Bulldogs.* Custom-made San Blas mola, print fabrics from Panama, cottons.

"I made this jacket in preparation for my 30th reunion of the Balboa (Panama) High School Class of 1964. Our school colors were red and white, but I decided to add other colors to keep the jacket from looking too boring. Some of the fabrics include Kuna shirt and scarf fabrics. It was a big hit at the reunion! Afterwards, the jacket won the Judge's Award for Special Creativity at the Logan Lap Quilters 12th Annual Quilt Show in Columbia, South Carolina."

Lesley Hendricks, *San Blas Muffies.* San Blas molitas, assorted cotton fabrics, beads, coins.

"I made these bears to commemorate a 1992 trip back to Panama with Balboa High School classmate Gail Ferrick. I have been collecting molas since I was a teenager, and used them in pillows, wall hangings, and clothing."

Anne Eastwood, *Hooked Mola Vest.*

Linda Robinson, *Tres Pajaros*. Commercial and hand-dyed cotton, San Blas mola. Appliqué, hand and machine quilting, embroidery. PHOTO: Craig Freas.

"I enjoy combining San Blas molas with my techniques to create colorful and varied wall quilts. My fascination with ethnic textiles has grown as I have traveled and studied the arts of other countries."

Jean Davidson, *Monarch Butterflies on Eucalyptus Leaves.*
Appliqué, reverse appliqué, embroidery.
PHOTO: **Tony Grant.**

"My botanical molas represent the Kuna design type classified as 'morganikat' or pictorial. This mola was sewn in honor of the annual migration of the butterflies that settle in the eucalyptus trees in special areas around the Monterey Bay in California."

Nancy Prichard,
Snowball.
Watercolor and handmade paper collage.

Jean Davidson, *Apple Blossom.* Appliqué, reverse appliqué, Seminole patchwork, embroidery.
PHOTO: **Tony Grant.**

"I used an apple blossom picked in the spring as the model for this mola. The apples were ready for harvest by the time I finished stitching."

Barbara Lydecker Crane, Mola Pillows. *San Blas molas,* pieced cotton prints.

"These floor pillows fill one corner of my newly built studio. They were a perfect project to work on during the noise and confusion of construction."

Barbara Lydecker Crane, *Night Journey*. Appliqué on cotton blend fabrics.

"Unlike the skillful Kuna women, I had to sketch and revise this design on paper before I was ready to cut into cloth. The cotton/polyester blends proved not to be the best choice, because they didn't hold the turned-under edge nearly as well as 100% cotton. After struggling with the many sharp angles of the design, I was filled with admiration for the Kunas' stitching ability, as well as their design sense."

Robinsunne, *Reverse Appliqué Angel.* Assorted fabrics, embroidery, beads.

Cari Connolly, *Potlatch Gift.* Cotton, metallic thread, buttons, beads, dyed raw sisal. Appliqué, reverse appliqué, quilting, beading, fringe work. Photo: Joey Eastman.

"The art work of Northwest coast Native Americans is very disciplined in line and form. Because their designs were often carved in relief, they lend themselves naturally to the mola technique—material removed in some places and built up in others. Potlatch Gift, with its killer whale, eagle, and bear totems, was inspired by a Tlingit design carved in yellow cedar; its button work is similar to Chilkat blankets."

Phyllis Christenson, *Elephant Walk.* San Blas mola, cotton fabrics; woven strip piecing.

Phyllis Christenson,
Birds of Paradise.
San Blas molas, cotton, silk, Japanese
fabrics;
1st Place winner at
the 1997 wearable
art conference,
Fiesta en Santa Fe.

"This 3/4 length coat incorporates three small molas from a recent trip to Panama. I used a variety of piecing methods, including log cabin, spiraling, and strip piecing."

Dewey Lee Cornay, *Mola Gumbo*. San Blas molas, Guatemalan cottons, ethnic batik fabrics, braid, beads. Mola Gumbo was the 1995-96 Fairfield Garment.

How to Make a Mola

Traditional molas are made with various appliqué techniques, including traditional or overlay appliqué, inlay appliqué, and reverse appliqué. In fact, molas are synonymous with appliqué, as well as with bright colors and geometric designs.

Traditional or overlay appliqué, derived from the French word for "apply," is a decorative effect achieved by applying different shapes and sizes of fabric to a background cloth. A cut-out fabric motif is attached, or overlaid, to the background, and then additional motifs or designs are stitched on top or on other areas of the background. The shapes and designs applied to fabrics can be nearly infinite, and range from geometrics to florals. Appliqué is often used to decorate ready-to-wear garments and home decorating items.

Reverse appliqué suggests the opposite or "reverse" of overlay appliqué and, technically, it is. Layers of fabric are stacked together and then shapes or designs are cut out of the upper layers to reveal the layers below.

Inlay appliqué means the fabric is inlaid or sandwiched between the other cloth layers. Small pieces of contrasting fabrics are sandwiched between the larger layers, and they appear as a background behind the "windows" cut open by reverse appliqué. This method makes economical use of limited cloth and creates the impression that a mola is made out of many more layers of fabric than it actually is. For example, a seven-color mola may be made of three full-size panels of fabric, with four other colors inlaid in different sections.

While many people believe that molas are made entirely of reverse appliqué, this is not the case. This understanding of mola-making technique stems from a 1963 needlework magazine article, in which the writer tried to interpret what the Kuna women were doing. In reality, mola-makers use several different forms of appliqué to construct the basic mola, including the three described above, and then they may further embellish it with various embroidery stitches. Most molas are made of two or three main layers of fabric. The appearance of additional layers is created with the inlay appliqué technique described above, and with overlay appliqué by applying motifs to empty spaces within the overall design.

The use of reverse appliqué to create an entire mola would be both wasteful of material and very difficult to accomplish. When fabric supplies are limited, stitchers and sewers must be ingenious as well as economical, devising ways to get a lot of design mileage out of scraps of material. Complete mola panels of reverse appliqué waste cloth because many areas of the lower fabric layers don't show; the only portions that do show are those that are revealed by cutting the top layers and turning under the edges. Molas made entirely of reverse appliqué also would be terribly difficult to stitch. Imagine a seven-color mola made entirely with the reverse appliqué technique. Cutting down through all the layers one by one, in increasingly intricate designs, and then turning the edges under and stitching them down would not only be incredibly challenging, but would result in a very bulky product.

The Kuna women are famous for their beautiful reverse appliqué work, and the misconception prevails that reverse appliqué is all they do. However, they should also be recognized for their other finely stitched appliqué and embroidery techniques.

In this chapter, the combination of appliqué methods employed by the Kuna Indian women to make molas is explained and illustrated. You will see for yourself that working with just a few full-size layers of fabric and then using overlay and inlay appliqué to supplement the colors and design is far easier than struggling with many layers of fabric and working in reverse all the way down to the base or foundation layer.

FABRICS

The Kuna women prefer smooth, tightly woven cotton fabrics dyed in many bright colors. If you are just beginning to make a mola by the traditional method, you will probably find that cotton yardage is easiest to work with. Look for closely woven fabrics such as pima cotton, poplin, broadcloth, and percale. Even calico, which is finished with a washable starch, will work, although it rarely comes in solid colors. The tight and even weave of the cotton makes it more manageable, easier to turn the edges under, and more likely to result in clean edges to the design. A heavier weight fabric, such as denim or sailcloth, can be used as the background or foundation layer. Its heavier weight will support the many stitches and heft of the upper layers.

If you are experimenting with more innovative approaches to mola-making, such as using fusible products to adhere the fabric layers or a sewing machine to finish the cut edges, your fabric choices are greater. In this case, textured fabrics and felt can be interesting to work with and delicate material can be stabilized or interfaced before stitching down. Experiment with novelty fabrics for desired effects.

Preshrink or otherwise pretreat the selected fabric depending on the finished item you will be making. If your goal is to create a washable wearable, you will want to pretreat all the fabrics that go into it, to prevent shrinkage as well as color bleeding, running, or

fading. Prewashing will also remove all sizing and other fabric finishes used in the manufacturing process. The Kuna women do not pretreat their fabrics, probably because of the extremely limited supply of water on the islands. Another reason may be that the fabric's crispness created by the sizing or starch finish makes it easier to turn under a sharp, clear edge.

COLORS

Traditional molas are made from primary colors and other bright hues, and in solids rather than prints. You can study the molas shown in this book for customary arrangements of color to guide you in your own selection. However, unless you are aiming for an accurate reproduction of a traditional mola, you can try out many different shades, patterns, and prints. Perhaps you want to create a batik effect—then choose ethnic prints for the main fabrics and accent them with solids. The opposite would give a completely different look—solids for the major design elements and prints for accent borders or small appliqué motifs.

Because stitching a mola is time-consuming, you should work out your color combination in advance, especially if you are just starting out. Play around with swatches of fabric or purchase some colored artists' papers to work out various color schemes. An alternative is to draw designs with colored pencils or markers to see how colors interact. However, fabric or paper will give a closer approximation to the color arrangement of the real-life mola. You might want to review the basic rules of color theory or look at a color wheel printed in most large dictionaries. This will remind you about which colors are primary and secondary, which ones are complementary, and what contrast effects can be achieved with different combinations.

Once you have chosen the fabrics and colors, arrange them in the same order that the mola will be stitched, to see if there is any "bleed-through" of dark shades showing through the lighter ones. This can be a problem if you are combining pastels and darks in the same piece. For example, if your top layer will be a

light yellow and the next layer down will be a bright peacock blue, make sure the contrast between the two is not so extreme that the folded-under edges of the yellow layer will show clearly against the blue. If the blue layer does show through, and you still want to use the yellow on top, baste or fuse a lightweight facing fabric to the wrong side of the yellow and trim away the seam allowances, so the turned-under edge will be a single layer of the yellow fabric.

TOOLS AND SUPPLIES

The tools and supplies you need for making a mola are simple, inexpensive, basic hand-sewing accessories. If you don't already own them, you can find everything you need in any fabric, sewing, or needlework shop or department.

Needles

For hand-sewing needles, look for fine, sharp points and small sizes for easy pulling through the fabric. Embroidery needles, sharps, or millinery needles can all be used. Needles come in different sizes and lengths; experiment with various types to find those that are comfortable and easy to sew with. They also differ in threading design—some have large eyes, while others have open tops for easy threading. Again, use the needle types you find easiest to handle.

Thimble

Some sewers wouldn't be caught dead using thimbles, while others swear by them. If your choice is to use one, look at the various models available for sewing and quilting, and pick the one that will protect you from injury. Among the thimbles out there are open-tip, wraparound, leather, textured heavy paper,

and plastic versions. Some thimble types can even help you push the fabric edge under when you are stitching it down to the layer below.

Scissors

Because you will be cutting through the layers of fabric in reverse appliqué and cutting out small, intricate appliqué shapes, it's crucial that your scissors be small, easy to manage, and extremely sharp. Special models manufactured for embroidery and scherenschnitte, or paper-cutting, feature very sharp points, while some appliqué scissors may be easier to manipulate between the layers of fabric. Try out the different models before you settle on anything.

Thread

Follow your own preference when shopping for thread. Some stitchers use only cotton thread, while others like cotton and polyester blends. Look for lightweight thread, as it will make the smallest, and therefore the most invisible, stitches. Try to match the threads with the fabrics as closely as possible. For example if you are stitching the yellow layer to the blue, use a yellow thread so it will disappear into the cloth. If you cannot match the thread exactly, get as close as possible or try the invisible threads that are available today. Invisible thread can be finicky to work with, but it may be the best choice for a hard-to-match material.

Basting aids

It is recommended that the stacked full-size mola panels be basted together around the outside edges and inlaid fabric patches be basted in position before cutting and stitching. Basting keeps everything securely in place and prevents stitching mishaps that may have to be ripped out later. You can use hand or machine basting for this step, or some of the new notions available from your local sewing center. These include basting tapes that hold layers temporarily in place and can be removed or washed out, and various fusible web products that adhere fabrics together temporarily or permanently.

Design tools

While many experienced Kuna stitchers work their mola designs in a free-form fashion, others trace or sketch the design on the fabric layer before cutting and stitching. Transferring the lines of your mola design to the fabric will ensure that dimensions are accurate and the design comes out the way you envisioned.

You can simply use a pencil or chalk marker to draw the outlines of a design you sketched previously on graph paper. Or explore the many new tools and accessories now on the market that make transferring faster, easier, and more precise. Air erasable pens and iron-on transfer pens eliminate the need to wash out or rub off pencil markings. Embroidery tracing paper and dressmaker's carbon with tracing wheel make quick work of marking design lines on the material. Or recycle your used sewing machine needles to stitch (unthreaded) along the design lines, punching through the pattern paper; then sprinkle powdered chalk through the punched holes to indicate the design on the fabric. A quick brush-off removes the loose chalk in a second. You can also use stencils and quilting templates for a tremendous variety of design motifs that can be easily traced onto the fabric.

Handy accessories

Other supplies you may already have on hand can be useful at different stages of making a mola. You may want to pin the turned-under edges of the fabric layers before hand sewing them down; in this case, look for pins that are very sharp and not so large that they get in the way. If you choose not to pin the turned-under edges in place, a wooden toothpick, skewer, or textured leather thimble can be helpful at turning under the raw edge as you go. A dot on the fingertip of that tacky glue they use for counting money and shuffling papers also eases the turning-under procedure. An iron will come in handy for lightly steaming the mola to keep its dimensions sure.

DESIGNING

As you have seen in the beginning sections of this book, ideas for mola designs can come from anywhere—the natural world, manmade objects, geometric abstractions, and your own creative imagination. Adapting a design for mola stitching, however, takes a little thought and planning. The lines and shapes within the design must be large enough and widely spaced enough to allow cutting and turning under the raw edges. In other words, an intricate drawing with very fine outlines will not work very well in a mola.

If you're just starting out, look for simple, basic shapes that will be easy to trace, cut out, and stitch. Simple animals, flower and leaf shapes, and bold geometrics are good beginning designs. You can sketch the design and enlarge it on a photocopier, or work out your idea on graph paper to the same scale as the finished mola. If you're uncomfortable with freehand drawing, look through books, including this one, for ideas you can adapt. Needlework pattern books, quilting templates, and graphic design books can all be good sources for ideas.

Once you've settled on a design, the next step is to transfer or trace it onto the mola fabric so you will know where to cut through the layers and turn the edges under. If you're satisfied with the arrangement and order of fabric colors, stack the full-size mola panels in order on top of the foundation layer and baste around all outside edges. Then, use any of the transfer or tracing tools mentioned above to sketch your design onto the top layer. You may also want to baste along both sides of each design outline, to keep everything in place as you cut and stitch; however, this is not really necessary if you work step-by-step in small areas. You are now ready to start your mola.

BASIC TECHNIQUES

You will begin with reverse appliqué by cutting into the top layer of fabric, between design lines, following your traced pattern. See Figure 1. Take care not to slice the lower layer or layers of fabric. Use the sharp tips of your scissors or a pin to lift the top layer away from those below, to make it easier to begin cutting. You may wish to slash all the appropriate design areas of the top layer at once, but it will probably be easier for you to work in small areas at a time.

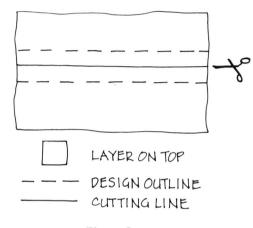

Figure 1
Cutting top layer

The raw edges on each side of the cut will be turned under and stitched down to the layer below. See Figure 2. Try to fold the edges under as little as possible, from 1/8" (3 mm) to no more than 1/4" (6 mm), to reduce bulk. You can use the tip of the needle, your fingertip, a toothpick, or your thimble to encourage the edges to turn under as you go. If you have traced the outlines of the design onto the fabric, it will be

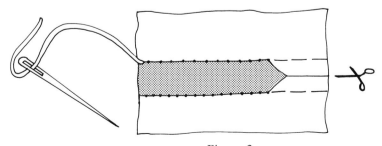

Figure 2
Turning under and stitching edges

clear where the foldline should be. Pin the folded edges down or hold them in place with your finger while you make the stitches.

Use a thread that closely matches the turned under fabric, space the hand stitches regularly, and make them as tiny as possible. If you work with short lengths of thread, the stitching will be easier to manage and the thread won't knot up. Bring the needle up from under the folded edge, move forward about 1/8" (3 mm), and catch a thread or two of the fabric beneath; bring needle up through the folded edge and continue. When you have completed stitching a section, pull the thread through the bottom or foundation layer and tie off.

The Kuna mola-makers make their tiny stitches from 1/16" (1.5 mm) to 1/8" (3 mm) apart; you should try for no further apart than 1/4" (6 mm). Any wider and the turned-under edge may not stay stitched down neatly. If you are not an experienced hand sewer, your stitches may look a bit irregular and clumsy, but don't worry—you will quickly get better with practice. Remember that the Kuna women have been doing this all their lives.

Once this step is completed, your original traced lines will frame the underneath color and you will begin to see your design forming. Continue to cut, fold, and stitch the outlines of your design in the top layer. Then, do the same through the next layer down, exposing the bottom or foundation panel. When the reverse appliqué sections are complete, you will supplement the design areas with overlay appliqué shapes and embellish the finished mola with embroidery stitches.

When you have practiced with a simple reverse appliqué mola, made from just two or three layers of fabric, you may be ready to experiment with additional layers by using the inlay appliqué method. After you have planned your design and color scheme, and before you baste the full-size mola panels together, you will want to sandwich the contrasting inlay swatches between the top and next layers of fabric and baste them in position. Then, they will be in place when you are ready to cut through the top layer to expose them. Alternatively, pin the full-size panels together instead of basting them. Unpin the layers when you are ready to add the inlay swatch, separating the layers where you need to; then re-pin the outer edges together and use reverse appliqué to expose the inlaid area.

CORNERS, CURVES, & POINTS

The basic techniques explained above are great for straight lines, but sooner or later your design will present you with some curved and shaped outlines that require a little bit of extra attention. The techniques described below are to be used for shaped areas in the reverse appliqué sections of your mola, as well as the overlay appliqué shapes you will attach to the mola after

completing the reverse appliqué. If you have done any sewing or pieced quilting, these methods will be familiar to you.

Inside and outside corners

You will encounter inside and outside corners in just about every geometric design. It's easy to learn how to stitch around them, so you won't have to search for designs that feature only rounded corners.

For an inside corner, clip diagonally to the foldline at the corner, turn under the edges on either side, and stitch in place. See Figure 3. If you clip right to the corner, the edges will turn under easier, the corner will be a true right angle, and it will lie flat. If you're worried about unraveling or raw thread ends showing at the corner, use the point of a pin to

Figure 3
Inside corner

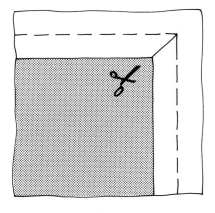

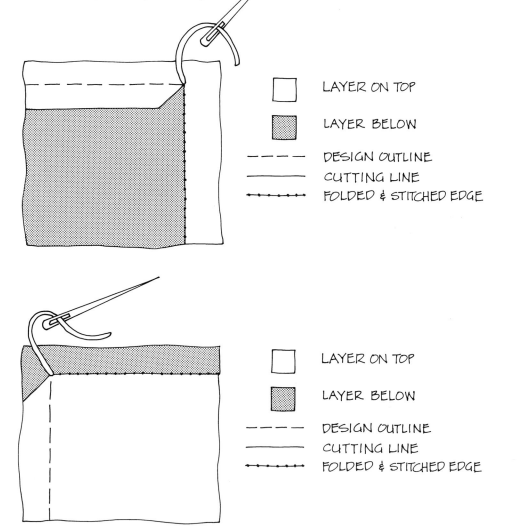

LAYER ON TOP

LAYER BELOW

- - - - DESIGN OUTLINE
———— CUTTING LINE
•—•—•—• FOLDED & STITCHED EDGE

Figure 4
Outside corner

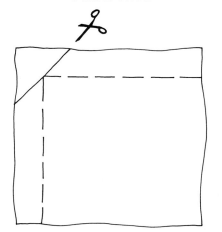

LAYER ON TOP

LAYER BELOW

- - - - DESIGN OUTLINE
———— CUTTING LINE
•—•—•—• FOLDED & STITCHED EDGE

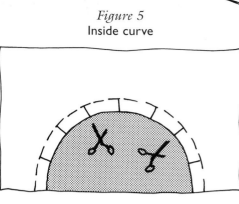

Figure 5
Inside curve

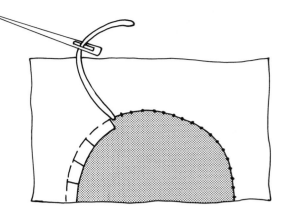

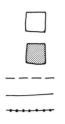

☐ LAYER ON TOP

▨ LAYER BELOW

– – – – DESIGN OUTLINE

——— CUTTING LINE

•••••• FOLDED & STITCHED

apply the tiniest drop of fray retardant to the clipped corner. Pretest the fray retardant on your fabric before you do this, to be sure you won't end up with a brittle spot or a stain.

For an outside corner, trim the fold-under allowance diagonally across where the corner point will be, turn under the edge along one side and stitch in place, then turn under the other edge and stitch in place. See Figure 4. Clip to within a thread or two of the corner point, for a sharp corner that will lie flat. Anchor the corner point with tiny stitches spaced even closer than usual.

Inside and outside curves

Very gentle curves may not require any clipping or trimming to get them to turn under and lie flat. You will be able to tell almost instantly if a curve is gentle enough to handle as is. However, if curves are sharp or the fabric is bulky, clipping and notching will help

you turn under the curved edges smoothly and will prevent puckering or stretching of the finished shape.

For an inside, or concave, curve, clip the seam allowance along the curve. Then, turn under the edge and stitch down. See Figure 5. For an outside, or convex, curve, notch the seam by clipping small triangles out of the allowance. Then, turn under the edge and stitch down. See Figure 6.

Points

Points are similar to corners, but are more extreme in their shape. As you did for the outside corner, you will clip diagonally across the outside tip of the point and then trim the seam allowance along each side edge of the point, tapering out to the original cutting line. Then, turn under the edges one by one and stitch down. See Figure 7. For the inside tip of the point, you will simply clip diagonally to the point, as you did for the inside corner, and turn under the edges for stitching.

Figure 6
Outside curve

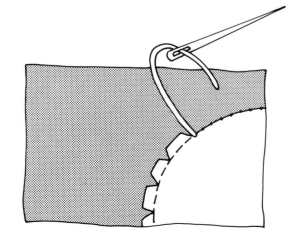

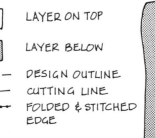

☐ LAYER ON TOP

▨ LAYER BELOW

– – – – DESIGN OUTLINE

——— CUTTING LINE

•••••• FOLDED & STITCHED EDGE

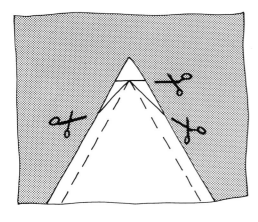

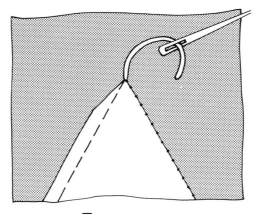

Figure 7
Points

LAYER ON TOP

LAYER BELOW

- - - - DESIGN OUTLINE

———— CUTTING LINE

•—•—•—• FOLDED & STITCHED EDGE

Sawtooth edge

A sawtooth edge looks complicated, but is really very easy to accomplish. You simply make a series of regularly spaced clips along a straight edge, then turn down the edges one at a time between each clip, to form a triangle or sawtooth shape. See Figure 8. Stitch each sawtooth edge before folding and stitching the next one, and anchor the point of each sawtooth with an extra tiny stitch or two.

Figure 8
Sawtooth edge

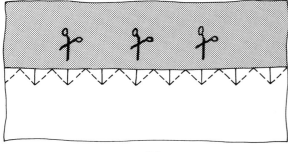

FINISHING

When you have completed both the reverse appliqué and appliqué sections of your design, evaluate the result and determine whether additional embroidery will enhance the overall effect. If so, now is the time to add it. The Kuna women use a few basic embroidery stitches, such as the running stitch and chain stitch, to add decorative details to the finished mola or accentuate specific design lines.

Use sewing thread or embroidery floss in coordinating or contrasting colors for this final step. You might want to lightly chalk the lines you will be embroidering, to ensure an accurate result. Depending on your preference, use an embroidery hoop to hold the fabric taut or just hold the mola in place with your hands. Try to keep your stitches consistent in size and spacing. When changing thread colors or finishing your stitching, pull the thread through the bottom layer and knot. See Figure 9 for how to do the running stitch and chain stitch.

When you completely finish with the stitching and embroidery, remove all basting threads or tapes and brush off any remaining chalk or pencil marks. Lightly press the mola from the back side to set all folds and restore the mola's shape. If you did not pretreat the fabrics and are not sure whether the colors will bleed, do not use steam when pressing. Instead, press with a dry iron.

You are now ready to incorporate your mola into a larger piece, such as a quilt or wearable jacket, back it with a plain fabric and stuff it for a pillow, or simply hang it up and admire your artistry.

TIPS FOR STITCHING SUCCESS

■ Good, strong lights will help you see what you're doing when folding under the cut edges and stitching them down. This will ensure small, evenly spaced, accurate stitches—and healthy eyes.

■ When doing any hand stitching, work in a comfortable position. Sit at a table or the kitchen counter, with the work on the surface in front of you. Or sit with a pillow in your lap to raise the mola to a good working height.

■ Cut and fold under the edges of your design in short distances, as you go. Working in small stretches prevents the fabric layers from rearranging themselves and helps you stay in control.

■ Match your thread as closely as possible to the fabric you're sewing down, so the stitches will not be obvious.

■ Use short pieces of thread, to prevent inconvenient knotting.

■ Urge the raw edges of the fabric to turn under with the tip of the needle, your fingertip, or other improvised "pusher."

■ Sew toward yourself, drawing the needle from the outside in toward you.

■ Clip inside curves, notch outside curves, and trim points so they will lie flat when stitched down.

■ Space stitches even closer together along curves, at points and corners, and around small intricate shapes.

■ If you want to start working with mola-inspired designs, without also having to practice your hand stitching techniques, get acquainted with the layers and color combinations by experimenting with cut paper or felt. See pages 48-65 for some easy projects that introduce you to the mola layers and design motifs.

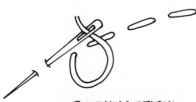

RUNNING STITCH   CHAIN STITCH

AN INSTRUCTOR'S TEACHING AID

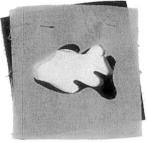

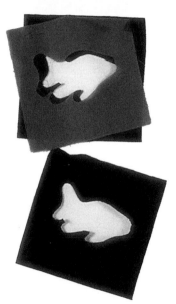

Jean Davidson is an enthusiastic lover of molas and an artist who has been inspired by molas (see her appliqué panels on page 31). She teaches classes in mola techniques at a local college and uses the demonstration panel shown here to illustrate how the Kuna women make mirror-image molas for the front and back of their blouses. It also shows how the Kunas get a lot of mileage out of limited supplies of fabric with their "waste-no-fabric" method of mola-making.

This teaching aid panel demonstrates how two similar molas can be made by swapping cut-out pieces from one to the other, thereby wasting no fabric. Turn the page for a row-by-row description of this method.

Row 1. The three-fabric stack at left has a textured red on the bottom, a smooth lightweight orange in the middle, and a lightweight black piece on top. The stack on the right has the same red on the bottom, a lightweight yellow in the middle, and the same black on top. A fish design is sketched on the tops of each stack and then cut along the outline. The edges of the fish are turned under and stitched down to the lower layers in the reverse appliqué technique. Note that a circle for the eye has been cut out of each fish, turned under, and stitched down.

Row 2. The black pieces remaining after cutting out the fish in Row 1 are set aside, exposing the middle layers of each stack. The same fish outline is cut through the orange and yellow middle layers, the edges turned under and stitched down.

Row 3. The remaining orange and yellow pieces from Row 2 are set aside with the leftover black pieces from Row 1. The red bottom layer of each stack is now the background for a black fish bordered by orange on the left, and yellow on the right. Note that tiny circles have been cut out of both fish eyes, the

edges turned under and stitched down, exposing a dot of the red foundation layer.

Row 4. The leftover orange and yellow pieces are swapped and laid down on top of the two stacks; the leftover black pieces remain set aside. The cut-out edges are turned under and stitched down to the foundation layer, creating a red outline around each fish.

Row 5. The leftover black pieces are now laid on top of the two stacks, the cut-out edges turned under and stitched down, to form a black frame around the multi-colored fish.

Row 6. While the two panels feature mirror-image multi-color fish, further embellishment is added to created related but non-identical mola panels. Additional reverse appliqué is worked in both panels to reveal the lower layers of fabric, and overlay appliqué is stitched on top to create even more layers of color. Chain-stitch embroidery is worked as a final step, to add visual interest and accentuate various design lines of the appliqué shapes.

The mola panel on this easy-to-make apron by Jean Davidson was one of two similar, but not identical, squares made with the waste-no-fabric method.

Cut-Paper Note Cards

DESIGNER:

Bobby Gold

THESE NOTE CARDS are an easy and fail-safe way to make colorful mola projects for fun gifts, or to use yourself. Experiment with different colors of novelty paper for very different effects.

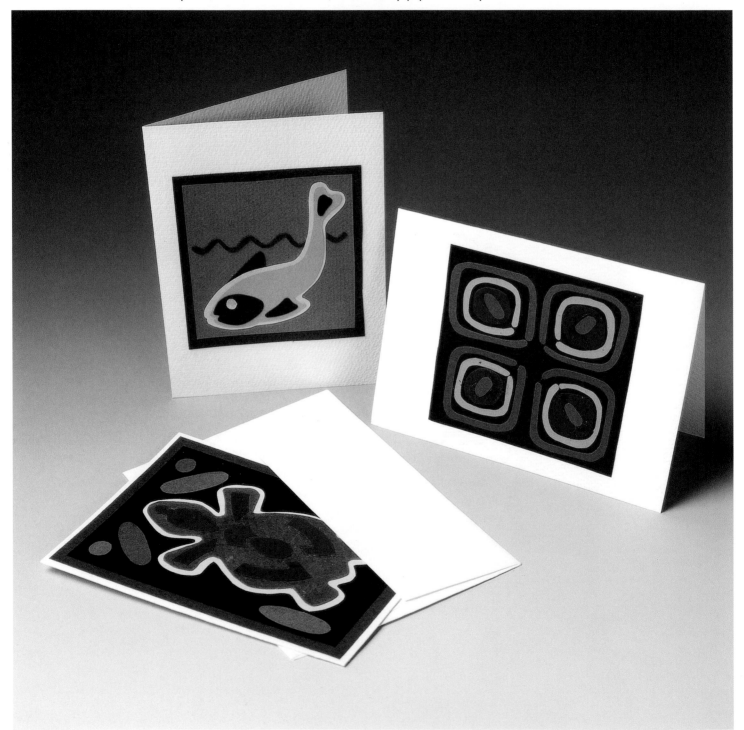

MATERIALS

- Ready-made note cards with matching envelopes, from stationery and office supply stores (or)

- 80 lb. watercolor paper or assorted colors of novelty paper from paper and art supply stores, in assorted weights up to construction paper weight

- Standard size envelopes in nice paper to coordinate with papers selected for cards

TOOLS AND SUPPLIES

- Craft knife or sharp scissors

- Adhesive stick, glue, or rubber cement

- Weight or heavy book

INSTRUCTIONS

1.

Trace, photocopy, or otherwise transfer the design shapes shown here to your selected papers.

2.

Cut out design shapes with scissors or craft knife.

3.

Cut out one or more background squares of slightly different sizes, so they will overlap nicely.

4.

Arrange design shapes on top of background square(s) until you get an effect you like.

5.

Carefully turn over stack of shapes.

6.

Apply glue or adhesive to back of each shape, one by one, and affix to front of card. Hand-press in place.

7.

When all shapes are affixed to card, cover card with heavy book or other weight and leave for several hours or overnight to set.

TIPS

- When using a craft knife to cut out shapes, a leftover piece of linoleum or a self-healing cutting mat will protect your tabletop surface.

- Experiment with different color effects, such as changing the colors of background squares only, the design shapes only, high contrast, low contrast, brights, and pastels. The possibilities are endless, and these cards are so quick to make that you can try lots of color schemes.

- Change the design arrangements for a vertical, side-opening card or a horizontal, bottom-opening card. They don't all have to open the same way.

- For creative gift-giving ideas, design groups of five or six cards in different themes, such as fish, leaf shapes, flowers, or geometrics. Then, package them in nicely wrapped or ribboned sets.

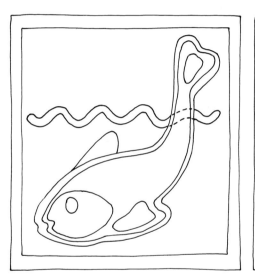

Tigger in the Sky Mola Collage

DESIGNER:

Nancy Prichard

LAYERS OF DIFFERENT PAPERS are painted and then stacked like fabrics to make this mola portrait of a favorite pet.

MATERIALS

- Handmade paper and/or cotton linter sheets from paper, crafts, or art supply stores

- Scrap paper for making pattern templates

- Spray fiber dyes and/or acrylic paints

- White glue

- Opaque colored markers

- Contrasting or coordinating thread

TOOLS & SUPPLIES

- Paper-cutting scissors

- Pinking shears

- Sewing machine

INSTRUCTIONS

1.

Gather several small sheets of handmade paper and/or cotton linter sheets. For the project shown here, the following sizes are needed:

- one piece for background border, 9 x 12" (23 x 30.5 cm)

- one piece for background, 8½ x 11½" (21.5 x 29 cm)

- three pieces for making cats and area around cats, 6 x 9" (15 x 23 cm)

- one piece for border around cats, 7 x 10" (18 x 25.5 cm)

- four or more pieces for border patterns and details, 3 x 4½" (7.5 x 11.5 cm)

2.

Using either acrylic paints or spray dyes, color the sheets of paper as desired. Brushes can be used to apply the acrylic paint; pump spray bottles work well for the dyes. The more dye you use, the more intense color you will get. All papers should be painted different colors, except the very small pieces, which can repeat the other colors.

3.

While papers are drying, sketch the cats or your design on scrap 6 x 9" (15 x 23 cm) paper. See Figure 1. Remember to keep the designs bold and simple. Cut out the design to use as the pattern template.

4.

When painted paper is dry, trace the cat or your own design on one of the 6 x 9" (15 x 23 cm) pieces. Reverse the design to make a mirror image, trace again, and cut out. See Figure 2.

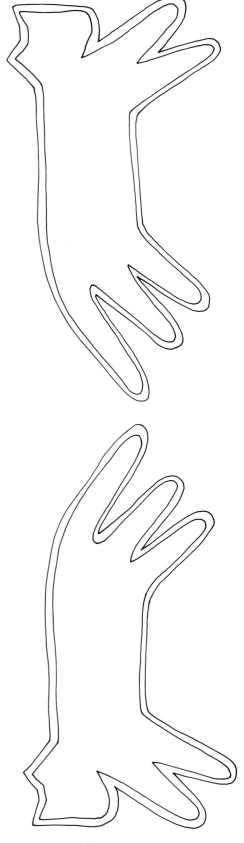

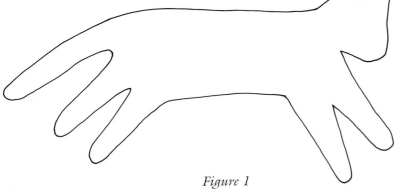

Figure 1
Enlarge 125%

Figure 2
Enlarge 125%

5.

Glue cats onto another 6 x 9" (15 x 23 cm) piece of painted paper. When glue is dry, carefully cut around the images, leaving ⅛ to ¼" (3 to 6 mm) of the second paper showing around the outside edge. See Figure 2.

6.

Glue cats onto the third 6 x 9" (15 x 23 cm) piece of painted paper, as shown in Figure 3.

7.

Cut two spiral sun shapes out of small pieces of painted paper. Stack and glue as in step #5. Glue sun shape between cats.

8.

Add a border behind the cats/sun panel, using the 7 x 10" (18 x 25.5 cm) paper. This can be machine stitched in place, or cut with pinking shears and glued to the back.

9.

Cut small stars and other shapes out of the paper scraps, layer and glue, and add to the background. See Figure 4.

10.

Use colored markers to outline the cat, sun, and other images, or to add dots, squiggles, and other accents to the background space. Another option is to use a squeeze bottle to apply paint accents.

11.

Glue the 8½ x 11½" (21.5 x 29 cm) background piece to the back and add various border patterns and shapes cut from the scrap pieces. See Figure 5.

12.

Mount the completed mola on the 9 x 12" (23 x 30.5 cm) background border piece and decorate the edges with crinkle-edge scissors or pinking shears.

TIPS

■ If you cannot find handmade paper or cotton linter, substitute any heavyweight, flexible. paper such as manila or construction paper. These substitutes should be painted with acrylic paint, because the paper colors are not light fast.

■ To create a more authentic mola look, choose bright, clear colors and keep designs simple and bold. But don't forget the real fun—the small details and surface embellishment.

■ Use fabrics instead of papers, for an entirely different look and feel. Just remember to stabilize or interface the fabric before painting and layering. Put the layers together with fabric glue or machine stitching.

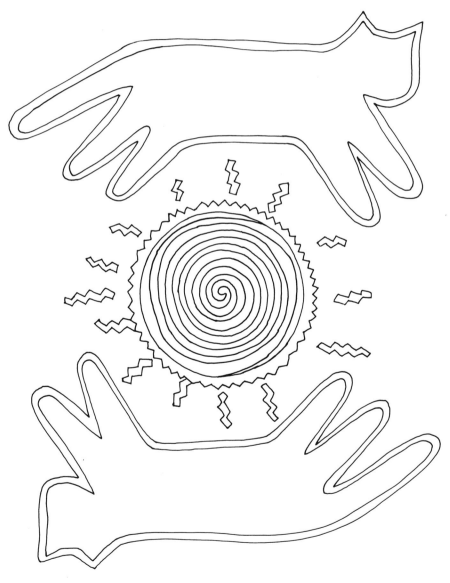

Figure 3
Enlarge 125%

Figure 4
Enlarge 125%

Figure 5
Enlarge 125%

Paper Molas

DESIGNER:

Robinsunne

CUT AND STACK DIFFERENT COLORS OF PAPER in mola-inspired designs for a fun way to create a basketful of small gifts, from window ornaments to bookmarks. These paper molas make a great classroom or club project.

MATERIALS

- Assorted papers of construction paper weight

TOOLS & SUPPLIES

- Craft knife or small, sharp paper-cutting scissors

- Adhesive stick, glue, or rubber cement

- Colored pencils

INSTRUCTIONS

1.

Trace the designs shown on the next page onto plain paper and experiment with colored pencils until you get a color scheme you like.

2.

Cut away sections of the design from each paper layer and overlay it on the layer below.

3.

Paste or glue the layers together, one at a time, and weight down with a heavy book for several hours.

For the hand:

1.

The red heart shape is the uncut bottom layer showing through the layers above.

2.

The next layer up is purple, with a heart shape cut out of the middle.

3.

The next layer up is lime green, which is trimmed around the heart shape and inside the fingers.

4.

The top layer is black, which is trimmed to form an outline around the hand.

For the bear:

1.

The black layer is cut along the lines of the maze and laid over the white background layer.

2.

The heart shape and mouth are trimmed out of the white background, and a patch of red paper is glued to the bottom.

TIPS

■ Working with a medium to heavy weight of paper makes it easier to manage the intricately cut layers. The layers also build up nicely, giving the finished project a lot of texture.

■ Don't try to glue every little part of the cut design; just use dabs on sections that are large enough so the glue won't ooze beyond the edges. A toothpick can place the tiniest drop of glue or paste exactly where you need it.

■ Wait until all the layers are stacked and glued before trimming the outside edge; then, all the layers will be precisely the same size and shape.

Mola Stencil Design

DESIGNER:

Jenni Bateman

THESE MOLA-INSPIRED STENCIL DESIGNS brighten up the examining rooms at the Timber Pointe Easter Seal Rehabilitation Center for children with disabilities in Hudson, Illinois. They're easy to make and are a great way to begin designing mola-inspired projects for your own home. The kids love them, and you will, too.

TOOLS & SUPPLIES

- Graph paper
- Colored pencils or crayons
- Blank stencil material
- Sharp craft knife
- Cutting surface or self-healing mat
- Masking tape
- Spray adhesive
- Stencil or jar paints, from a craft supply store
- Stencil brushes, one for each color
- Paint tray
- Paper towels
- Permanent markers

INSTRUCTIONS

1.

Sketch different designs or enlarge and trace those shown here onto graph paper. You can also refer to the many stencil design books available at craft supply stores for ideas.

2.

Use colored pencils or crayons to indicate which design lines should be which colors.

3.

Tape color-coded stencil design to cutting surface.

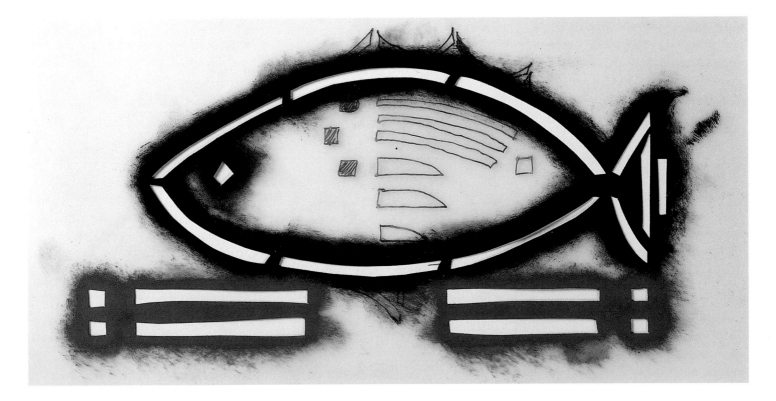

4.

Place first layer of blank stencil material on top and tape down. With craft knife, follow the color coding to cut only the areas for the first color. Remove stencil and set aside.

5.

Place second layer of blank stencil material on top, tape down. Repeat as above, cutting only the areas for the second color.

6.

Continue in this manner until all colors are cut from separate stencil blanks.

7.

Spray a light coating of adhesive on the back side of the cut stencils and let dry. The adhesive will allow you to reposition the stencil several times and will hold the stencil close to the surface you will be painting so that paint will not bleed under the stencil. Do not put the sprayed stencil patterns on any paper surface because they will bond to the paper.

8.

Position first stencil layer on surface to be painted.

9.

Arrange a small teaspoon of paint on paint tray. Dab a slightly moistened brush in paint and smudge off excess onto paper towel.

10.

In a circular or back and forth motion, apply paint to cut-out areas of stencil. Gently peel back stencil and check that the color is strong enough. Also check to see if the paint bled outside the lines, and if you used too much or too little paint.

11.

After a few moments of drying time, position second stencil layer on surface and apply second color, using a fresh brush.

12.

Repeat process until design is finished.

13.

With permanent markers, add some of the distinctive mola design lines and details to the stenciled pattern.

TIPS

■ When designing your stencil, keep the shapes very simple so they will be easy to cut and paint. Circles, squares, and rectangles are a great way to begin.

■ Practice painting on a sample board first, to test your color scheme and get acquainted with how much paint you need to apply for the best effect. Remember, too much paint will bleed behind the stencil, smudging lines and leaving unwanted blots of color.

■ You can stencil just about anything! Experiment with fabric paints on cloth for garments and window treatments, stencil the backsplash areas behind your bathroom and kitchen sinks, or paint accent designs on your walls or floors. You can even use epoxy paints on plain ceramic tiles, for hot plates to use at the dinner table or give as gifts.

Mola Portfolio Cover

DESIGNER:

Teresa Pla Belio

CREATE A CUSTOM BINDER with unique mola designs to hold your resumé, photo scrapbook, personal journal, design portfolio, or sheets of art paper to give to someone special. It's easy, quick, and much more interesting than a store-bought portfolio!

MATERIALS

- Assorted sizes and textures of paper in different colors

- Two pieces of cardboard, 10 x 13" (25.5 x 33 cm)

- One piece of sturdy medium-weight paper, 21¾" x 14½" (55 x 37 cm)

- One piece of interesting lightweight paper, 20¼ x 13" (51.5 x 33 cm)

- Approximately 1½ yards (1.4 m) ribbon, ⅜" (1 cm) wide

TOOLS & SUPPLIES

- Craft knife or scissors

- Adhesive stick, glue, or rubber cement

- Weight or heavy book

INSTRUCTIONS

1.

Cut and arrange shapes out of assorted textures and colors of paper to form two designs that are no larger than the cardboard pieces, but can be smaller.

2.

Glue the design layers to each other, one by one, starting from the bottom. After affixing each layer, put a weight on top for several hours to make sure the layers stay well-attached to one another before gluing on the next layer.

3.

When the mola designs are completed, paste them to the sturdy medium-weight paper in the front and back cover positions, leaving a 3/4" (2 cm) border all around and a 1/4" (6 mm) gap in between. See Figure 1.

4.

Position the cardboard pieces on the back side of the mola designs, leaving a 3/4" (2 cm) border all around and a 1/4" (6 mm) gap in between; glue or paste in place.

5.

Apply paste or glue to the back side of the border and fold to inside, around the outside edges of the cardboard pieces. Place weights on top for several hours, to set.

6.

Cut ribbon into six pieces, approximately 9" (23 cm) long.

7.

Cut slots for ribbon at desired spots, insert ends of ribbon and glue to inside. See Figure 2.

8.

Paste or glue sheet of interesting paper to inside, covering the ribbon ends, cardboard pieces, and border edges. Place weights on top for several hours or overnight.

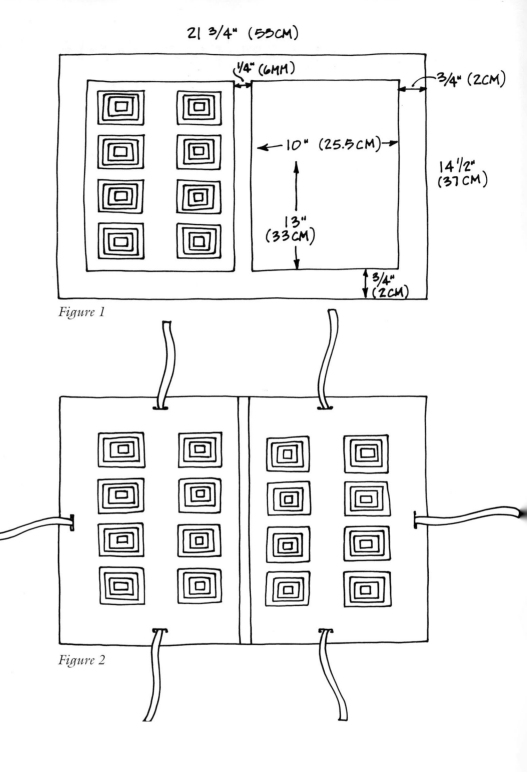

Figure 1

Figure 2

TIPS

■ You don't need to buy lots of new paper for this project. If you have just little scraps of different papers, recycle them into a beautiful piecework design.

■ Be creative with your selection of the paper for the inside. It can be marbleized art paper, interesting home decorating wallpaper, or unusual gift-wrapping paper.

■ Use fabric, leather, or suede for a completely different texture to your mola design.

Mola-Inspired Felt Ornaments

DESIGNER:

Pat Samuels

MAKE A BIG IMPACT WITHOUT A LOT OF WORK when you decorate the house or wrap up packages with these mola-inspired trimmings. Playing with bright colors and fun patterns will really get your imagination going.

MATERIALS

for approximately 12 ornaments in various sizes

- ½ yard (.5 m) black cotton fabric

- ¼ yard (.25 m) pieces of bright solid-colored cotton fabrics (red, blue, green, orange, gold, purple, red, etc.)

- ½ yard (.5 m) red felt

- 2 yards (1.85 m) fusible web product

- 2 yards (1.85 m) red trim (rickrack, ribbon, or cord)

- 1 spool red rayon machine embroidery thread

- 1 spool red regular machine thread

TOOLS & SUPPLIES

- Sewing machine with zigzag stitch

- Small sharp-pointed scissors

- Pinking shears

- Quilter's ruler and rotary cutter (or) paper templates in 2" (5 cm), 3" (7.5 cm), and 4" (10 cm) sizes

- Fray retardant

INSTRUCTIONS

1.

Press all fabrics to remove wrinkles and folds.

2.

Cut fusible web product slightly smaller than the ¼ yard (.25 m) pieces of assorted fabrics and fuse to the wrong sides, following manufacturer's instructions. When fabrics have cooled, peel off the web's paper backing.

3.
Cut 2" (5 cm), 3" (7.5 cm), and 4" (10 cm) squares out of the black fabric, using a rotary cutter and quilter's ruler or templates cut out of cardboard or heavy paper.

4.
Cut various shapes and lines out of the assorted fabrics and arrange them on the black squares, being sure to keep the fusible web's adhesive side down. Trace the designs shown here or have fun and experiment with your own shapes.

5.
Layer the cut shapes on top of one another, in brightly contrasting color arrangements for that distinctive mola look.

6.
When you are satisfied with the design, carefully lift the square to your ironing board. Lay a muslin pressing cloth gently on top and press to fuse the layers together, following the fusible web manufacturer's instructions. Do not move the iron around, as this will shift the position of the pieces.

7.
Place the fused design square on top of a piece of red felt that has been cut ½" (1.25 cm) larger all around. With regular sewing thread in the bobbin and rayon thread on top, attach with a zigzag stitch; the rayon thread will give a nice shiny effect.

8.
Trim outside edges of felt square with pinking shears.

9.
Cut a 9" (23 cm) piece of trim and attach to the back side of the ornament with a machine straight stitch. Seal the ends of the trim with a drop of fray retardant.

TIPS

■ Start with simple designs and then get as complex as you desire. It's so easy to arrange and rearrange the fabric shapes before you fuse them in place.

■ These little molas can be colorful building blocks of a larger creation, such as a decorative mobile that sways in the breeze, or small creations, such as hair ornaments and pins.

Café Mola

DESIGNER:

Clare M. Murray

THE DESIGN OF THIS HANGING WAS INSPIRED by the drawings and paintings of chairs by famous painters Georges Braque and Vincent Van Gogh. The technique was inspired by colorful molas. The combination is distinctively individual and easy to do—all stitched by machine, with raw edges showing for texture.

MATERIALS

- Assorted cotton and cotton blend fabrics, at least ¼ yard (.25 m) each

- Assorted sheer fabric for overlays

- Matching or contrasting thread

TOOLS & SUPPLIES

- Photocopier

- Sewing machine

- Sharp-pointed scissors and pins

- Chalk marker

INSTRUCTIONS

1.

Enlarge the drawing shown here to your desired size. The designer made a 6 x 12" (15 x 30.5 cm) drawing and enlarged it at 175%, to 11 x 22" (28 x 56 cm). With the added borders, the finished mola panel shown here is 16 x 26" (40.5 x 66 cm).

2.

Make several copies of the enlargement to cut up and use as pattern pieces or templates.

3.

Using one enlargement as a pattern, cut and piece together the two walls and the floor. The walls extend from the top of the awning, through the baseboards, to the floor. Machine stitch all seams, and let the raw edges show. If you want clean-finished seams, be sure to add seam allowances to all shapes when you cut them out.

4.

For the baseboards, cut the baseboard shape out of one of the photocopies and place it on the selected fabric. Cut out about ½" (1.25 cm) larger all the way around and pin to the back side of the wall/floor piece. Working on the back side, mark along the top edge of the baseboard pattern with chalk and indicate the line where the floor meets the wall. Machine stitch along the marked lines. Cut away the top layer of fabric to reveal the baseboard layer.

5.

For the windows, cut a piece of fabric larger than the area of all four windows and pin to the back of the panel. On the front, trace or draw the window shapes and stitch along traced lines. Cut away top layer. Repeat, for double-layer windows. Stack assorted sizes and shapes of sheer fabrics over top of the windows, as desired, and machine stitch down.

6.

For the sky, use a fabric with a star design and assorted sheers cut into smaller shapes. Stack fabrics as desired and stitch to top edge of mola panel.

7.

For the awning, use one of the photocopies to trace and cut out the awning shape. Stitch it on top of the panel, to connect the sky and wall sections.

8.

For the floor, use the chalk to sketch or trace floor pattern onto front of mola panel. Cut a piece of fabric large enough to cover entire floor area and baste to back side of panel. Stitch along the marked pattern and cut away the top layer to reveal the layer underneath.

9.

For the chair, cut out three fabric rectangles that are a little bigger than the area of the chair, stack them in the order desired, and baste on top of the mola panel. Draw or trace the chair design onto the top layer and stitch along the marked lines. Cut away one or more of the top fabric layers as desired, to reveal the layers below. Take care to not cut through the bottom layer. Stitch assorted small shapes of sheer fabrics on top, as desired.

10.

For the table, follow the same procedure that you did for the chair.

11.

For the top and side borders, cut three different fabrics into strips of 3 x 22" (7.5 x 56 cm) and layer them together. Attach the two side borders to the mola panel first, and then the top border. Stitch with wrong sides together in ¼" (6 mm) seam allowances; trim to ⅛" (3 mm), so raw edges will stand up on right side of panel.

12.

With chalk or pencil, extend some of the lines from the center part of the mola out onto the borders, such as the awning curve, baseboard lines, and floor markings. Stitch along these lines and cut away the layers of fabric as desired, to reveal the layers below. Add smaller shapes of sheer fabrics on top, as desired.

13.

For the backing, cut two layers of fabric, each one a little larger than the completed top. Place the mola panel on top of the two backing layers and stitch together around the outside edges. Trim a bit of raw edge away from the upper backing layer, to create a graduated border of different fabrics.

14.

Add a rod pocket on back, for hanging the completed mola panel on the wall.

Tips

■ Sheer fabrics enhance the layered effect of the appliqué technique, because they constitute a mola layer by themselves and, at the same time, are transparent enough to show the layers below. They also add a subtle sense of depth and interesting shadow quality.

■ Think of machine stitching as painting on fabric. The lines of stitching are a lot like the brush strokes and pencil lines of an artist, while small appliqué shapes are like dabs of oil paint on canvas.

A Family of Molas

DESIGNER:

Laura Elizabeth Green

IN TRUE MOLA-MAKER'S FASHION, you can create an entire family of mola projects, using the scraps left from one to make another so nothing is wasted! Modern convenience materials speed up the process—perfect if your time is limited.

Twelve-Flower Mola

This pretty picture will be framed, so no sewing is required! The leftover pieces from this one project can be made into five smaller molas—frame them as companion pieces to the large mola or give them as special gifts.

MATERIALS

- Cotton fabric in the following sizes and colors:

- blue, $13\frac{1}{2}$ x 17" (34 x 43 cm)

- red, 14 x $17\frac{1}{2}$" (35.5 x 44.5 cm)

- red, 9 x 9" (23 x 23 cm)

- pink, $14\frac{1}{2}$ x 18" (37 x 45.5 cm)

- pink, 9 x 9" (23 x 23 cm)

- purple, $15\frac{1}{2}$ x 19" (39.5 x 48.5 cm)

- green, 9 x 9" (23 x 23 cm)

- yellow, 9 x 9" (23 x 23 cm)

- 2 yards (1.85 m) fusible web product

TOOLS & SUPPLIES

- Black laundry marker
- Sharp-pointed scissors
- Iron

INSTRUCTIONS

To make the twelve flowers:

1.
Cut three squares of fusible web, approximately 9 x 9" (23 x 23 cm).

2.
Trace the pattern for the four flowers onto the paper backing of each square with a marker. The paper backing is transparent, so you can see through it to make tracing easier.

3.
Iron one square of fusible web to the wrong side of the yellow fabric, one square to the red fabric, and one square to the pink.

4.
Cut around each flower.

5.
Cut along the inner pattern lines of each flower, using the sharp-pointed scissors to snip into the fabric. You will use the leftover pieces to make the small molas. For example, in flower patterns A, B, and C, the odd-numbered pieces will make one full-size flower and the even-numbered pieces will make another smaller flower.

6.
Trace each leaf pattern several times onto fusible web, iron to the green fabric, and cut them out. Make a few purple leaves, too, for accent.

To make the background and borders:

1.
Cut a rectangle of fusible web approximately $13\frac{1}{2}$ x 17" (34 x 43 cm). Remove the paper backing and fuse to the wrong side of the blue fabric rectangle. Trim fused rectangle to $12\frac{1}{2}$ x 16" (31.5 x 40.5 cm).

2.
Cut a rectangle of fusible web approximately 14 x $17\frac{1}{2}$" (35.5 x 44.5 cm) and fuse to the wrong side of the red fabric rectangle. Trim to 13 x $16\frac{1}{2}$" (33 x 42 cm).

3.
Cut a rectangle of fusible web approximately $14\frac{1}{2}$ x 18" (37 x 45.5 cm) and fuse to the wrong side of the pink fabric rectangle. Trim to $13\frac{1}{2}$ x 17" (34 x 43 cm).

4.
Trim the blue rectangle to $12\frac{1}{2}$ x 16" (31.5 x 40.5 cm). Remove the paper backing and iron it on top of the red rectangle.

5.
Trim the red rectangle so that a $\frac{1}{4}$" (6 mm) border frames the blue background on all four sides. Remove the paper backing and iron on top of the pink rectangle.

6.
Trim the pink rectangle so that a $\frac{1}{4}$" (6 mm) border shows all around. Remove the paper backing and iron on top of the purple rectangle.

7.
Trim the purple rectangle so that a $\frac{1}{2}$" (1.25 cm) border frames the picture.

To assemble the twelve-flower mola:

1.
Arrange the twelve flowers on the background fabric. When you are pleased with the arrangement, remove the paper backing and fuse them in place.

2.
Arrange the leaves around the flowers and fuse in place.

3.
Frame the mola or satin stitch around the border's raw edges.

Small molas

Use the fabric pieces left over from the twelve-flower mola to make these small versions.

INSTRUCTIONS

1.
Iron a rectangle of fusible web to the wrong side of the selected background fabric and trim to approximately $5\frac{1}{2}$ x 7" (14 x 18 cm).

2.
Arrange the leftover scraps from about three large flowers and a few leaves on the background fabric.

5.

Cut sheets of heavyweight 8½ x 11" (21.5 x 28 cm) paper in half and fold in half to make two cards per sheet. Ask your printing vendor for nice colors of heavy paper, such as vellum bristol and other card stock.

6.

With an adhesive stick or glue, attach the color copies to the fronts of the cards.

7.

Purchase standard 4⅜ x 5¾" (11.3 x 14.5 cm) envelopes at the print shop or an office supply store.

Mola appliqué shirts

Here's a quick and inexpensive way to decorate T-shirts for the whole family. Just cut out the shapes and fuse them to the shirt—what could be simpler?

INSTRUCTIONS

1.

Wash, dry, and iron both the appliqué fabric and the shirt so they will not shrink later.

2.

Iron fusible web to the wrong side of the appliqué fabric pieces. Remove the paper backing and fuse them to the shirt in an arrangement you like.

3.

Iron a tear-away stabilizer to the wrong side of the shirt, to support the area that will be appliquéd.

4.

Satin stitch around the edges of the appliqué shapes.

5.

Tear away the stabilizer from the wrong side of the appliquéd area.

3.

When you are satisfied with the arrangement, remove the paper backing and fuse the flowers and leaves in place.

4.

Remove the paper backing from the assembled mola and fuse it to the fabric you have chosen as the border. Trim the border to about ¼" (6 mm) on each side. Add a second border if you like.

Mola note cards

Take advantage of your local print shop's color copier to make dozens of inexpensive note cards from your mola pictures.

INSTRUCTIONS

1.

At your local print shop, request that your mola picture be reduced so that the resulting copies are 3¾ x 5" (9.5 x 12.5 cm) or smaller; the finished cards will then fit into standard-size envelopes. Have four copies made on the color copier.

2.

Trim away the blank paper around each picture.

3.

Glue the copies on one sheet of 8½ x 11" (21.5 x 28 cm) paper. Color copiers cannot print all the way to the edges, so leave a ¼" (6 mm) frame all around.

4.

You will save money by copying four pictures at once. Make as many copies as desired and trim around each picture.

FLOWER A

FLOWER B

FLOWER C

FLOWER D

LEAVES

The mola pattern is designed so that the leftover pieces of fabric will make another pattern. The smaller flower at right is made from the pieces cut out of the larger flower at left.

Paper-Cut Mola Panels

DESIGNER:

Robinsunne

AN EASY PAPER FOLDING AND CUTTING technique makes it simple to design these pretty fabric panels. Stitch them on the sewing machine and then embellish them with beads and jewels for an effect like stained glass.

MATERIALS

- Scrap paper recycled from magazines or brochures

- Cotton or cotton blend tightly woven fabrics, 12" (30.5 cm) squares of three different colors

- Matching or contrasting thread

TOOLS & SUPPLIES

- Sharp-pointed scissors for cutting the designs, such as embroidery or cutwork scissors

- Invisible tape

- Chalk or disappearing ink marker

- Sewing machine, with darning foot, if available

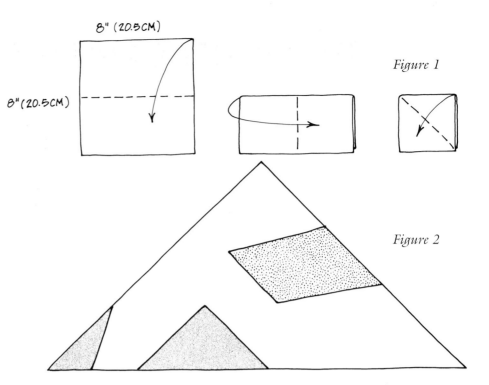

8" (20.5CM)

8" (20.5CM)

Figure 1

Figure 2

INSTRUCTIONS

To make the pattern template:

1.
Cut the scrap paper into 8" (20.5 cm) squares.

2.
Fold the paper in half, in half again, and in half once more to form a triangle. See Figure 1. The more precise and even you fold the paper, the more symmetrical the design will be.

3.
Make three or four chunky cuts into the folded paper triangle, cutting in from all of the edges or from just one or two of the edges. Do not make the design shapes too intricate. For the paper mola shown here, trace and cut the design shown in Figure 2.

4.
Open the paper-cut pattern and flatten or press with a dry iron.

To make the mola:

1.
Pin the fabric squares together in the top-to-bottom order you like best.

2.
Tape the paper-cut pattern to the top of the fabric stack. Do not tape across curves, corners, or other complex lines, because your pattern tracing will not penetrate the tape and you will not be able to see these important points. Instead, tape across straight lines; it will be easier to fill in the gaps under the tape.

3.
Trace the outline of the paper cutting onto the fabric with the chalk or disappearing ink marker.

4.
Remove the paper pattern and fill in any missing parts of lines that were hidden under the tape.

5.
Set your sewing machine for free-motion sewing by dropping or covering the feed dogs. Shorten the stitch length a bit and use a darning foot, if available, to reduce pressure on the fabric while sewing.

6.
With matching or contrasting thread, depending on the effect you want, sew the stacked fabric along the traced lines of your paper-cut design. Start in the middle of the fabric square and move outward. Instead of cutting the thread and restarting from shape to shape, lift the presser foot and move forward to the next shape; trim the traveling threads between shapes after stitching is completed.

7.
With small sharp-pointed scissors, carefully cut out the top layer of fabric between the lines of stitching. You can decide to cut out the small "windows" within small shapes, as in the squares and center star of the mola shown here,

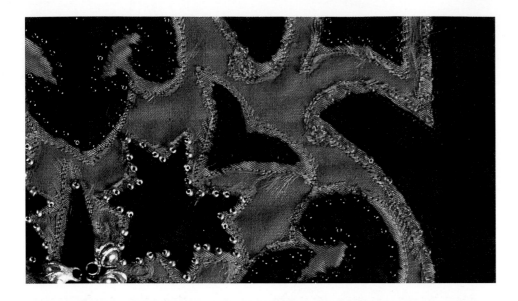

or leave them in place. Take care not to cut into the lower layers of fabric.

8.

Change thread colors, if desired, and sew around the shapes you just cut, about ⅛" (3 mm) away from the raw edges.

9.

Carefully cut out the middle layer of fabric between the lines of new stitching, to reveal the bottom layer. You might want to leave the outside border area uncut, as in the mola shown here.

10.

Press the completed mola and hem or otherwise edge it.

11.

Embellish as desired with hand embroidery, decorative machine embroidery, beads, buttons, feathers, gems, etc.

12.

Use the mola by itself as a wallhanging or incorporate it into a pillow, tote bag, or wearable item.

TIPS

■ Use scrap paper to make lots of paper cuts, and then choose the ones you like best. With recycled sheets, you won't feel like you're wasting paper during this experimentation stage.

■ Free-motion stitching is a lot like drawing and so much more fun. Try it with or without an embroidery hoop and use your hands to guide the fabric.

■ Use a lightweight fusible web on the back side of the fabric layers to minimize fraying. This is especially effective for loosely woven materials.

■ If the size and shape of the cuts in the paper pattern are big and bold, you can use up to five layers of fabric. The effect is beautiful, like a kaleidoscope.

Mola Wallhanging

DESIGNER:

Lori Kerr

PAINT A PICTURE of the natural world in appliqué flora and fauna shapes. Then hang it on the wall as a reminder of the colorful world we live in.

MATERIALS

- Assorted fabrics in prints and solids
- Double-faced fusible stabilizer
- Matching and contrasting thread
- Rayon machine embroidery thread in contrasting or variegated colors
- Drawings of plants, animals, and birds from photographs or of your own design
- Heavyweight paper, such as construction paper

TOOLS & SUPPLIES

- Sewing machine
- Iron
- Scissors
- Chalk marker

INSTRUCTIONS

1.

Draw or photocopy flora and fauna shapes, enlarging or reducing until you get the size you want. Trace the photocopied shapes or the bird, squirrel, insect, frog, and fish designs shown here onto heavyweight paper, to use as pattern templates.

2.

Iron stabilizer to wrong side of fabric pieces you will use for the animal shapes.

3.

Transfer animal patterns onto stabilizer side and cut shapes out of fabric.

4.

Peel backing away and fuse shapes to fabrics selected as background borders. Trim background fabric to create a border of approximately 1/4" (6 mm) around each animal.

5.

Repeat, fusing each shape to a third layer of fabric and trimming to create a border around each one.

6.

Cut a circle for the center of the sun and fuse to two larger background circles, as above. Cut some narrow strips of fabric to use for the sun's rays. Set animal shapes and sun components aside.

7.

Choose three fabrics for the background sky, earth, and water. Stitch

together end-to-end to form a three-part background; the three parts do not have to be equal in length. The finished size of the sky/earth/water background of the wallhanging shown here is 50" (127 cm) long and 18" (45.5 cm) wide.

8.

Arrange the three-layer animals and sun components on the background, as desired, and pin in place.

9.

With chalk, draw approximate size and placement of bars around each shape. When satisfied with distribution and appearance of overall pattern, sew the animals and sun to the background with the rayon embroidery thread, using a machine blanket stitch, zigzag stitch, or satin stitch.

10.

Cut strips of fabric and machine stitch to the background according to chalk marks.

11.

Trim background to an even rectangle, if necessary. Choose a contrasting fabric and attach a wide

border to the four sides; the black border in the wallhanging shown here is 5" (12.5 cm) wide, plus seam allowances.

12.

Cut contrasting fabric bars of varying lengths and widths, and sew to border.

13.

Machine quilt the border in a stipple, channel, or random design, using invisible nylon thread (as in the wallhanging shown here), contrasting thread, or variegated thread.

14.

Bind the raw edges of the wallhanging with a narrow band of contrasting print or solid fabric.

15.

Add a rod pocket or loops to the back side, for hanging on the wall. Attach weights to the bottom edge, if needed for finished work to hang properly.

TIPS

■ Traditional molas fill all available space with appliqué shapes and other embroidery. Once you have attached the main design shapes, evaluate the space remaining in the background and the border for creative additions of color and texture.

"Guess Who's Coming to Dinner" Table Dressing

DESIGNER:

Vicki Gadberry

DRESS UP YOUR DINNER TABLE with a collection of bright molas for a surprising and innovative interior decorating touch. The printed fabric piecework showcases these beautiful molas to their best advantage.

- Assorted molas of approximately the same size, in varying design themes and colors

- Assorted print and solid fabrics for pieced borders and backing, ½ to 1 yard (.5 to .95 m) of each

- Black fabric for frame around each mola, 1 to 1½ yards (.95 to 1.4 m)

TOOLS & SUPPLIES

- Graph paper and colored pencils

- Sewing machine

INSTRUCTIONS

1.

Decide how many molas you want to incorporate into the table dressing and measure each one; in the project shown here, the molas were all approximately 15 x 12" (38 x 30.5 cm). Depending on the size of the molas, the measurements of each one's surrounding borders may vary, to result in an even-sized table runner.

2.

On graph paper, sketch the size of each mola and draw different border arrangements until you arrive at one you like. See Figure 1. The plan for the project shown here went through six revisions before any fabric was cut.

3.

Add to final sketch all measurements, including length and width of molas and border strips, to result in the final desired size for your table.

4.

Prewash all fabrics for piecing, to preshrink and remove any sizing. Press wrinkles out before cutting into strips.

5.

Lay out molas with fabrics to be used

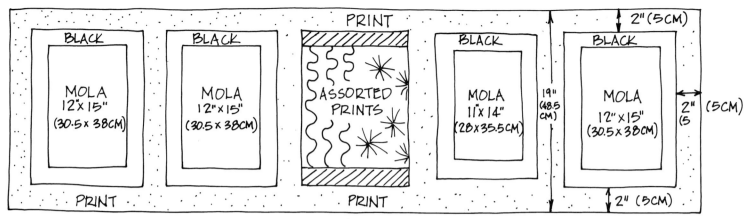

Figure 1

for borders; stand back and evaluate how the colors and patterns interact; rearrange placement as desired.

6.

Cut strips of assorted fabrics to sizes planned in sketch, adding ½" (1.25 cm) seam allowances to all edges.

7.

Stitch black frame pieces to all molas, using ½" (1.25 cm) seams. Press seams open.

8.

Arrange molas in desired sequence. Connect and edge them with pieced border strips, using ½" (1.25 cm) seams. Press all seams open after stitching.

9.

To cover back side of table runner, cut and arrange assorted fabric pieces in a pleasing pattern, allowing for ½" (1.25 cm) seams. Stitch and press all seams open.

10.

With right sides together, stitch backing to table runner around all edges, leaving an opening large enough to turn the whole piece to the right side. Trim, turn, press, and hand stitch opening.

11.

For the shorter crosspiece, create two framed and edged mola panels as above. Sew pieced backing to each mola, as in step #10, but leave a large opening on the fourth edge.

12.

For the insert, cut two pieces of coordinating fabric as long as the main table runner is wide, plus ½" (1.25 cm) seam allowances at each end. With right sides together, stitch pieces together along the lengthwise edges, leaving the ends unstitched. Trim, turn, and press.

13.

Slip the ends of the insert into the crosspiece openings and stitch along seamlines. See Figure 2. Hand stitch any remaining opening in crosspiece.

14.

Place crosspiece on table first, then position longer runner on top, covering insert.

TIPS

■ When you are sketching ideas for the table runner on graph paper, remember that printed fabric will look "busier" when stitched together than when sketched on paper. Therefore, try to keep the pieced design fairly simple. The borders should showcase and set off the molas, not compete with them.

■ Different combinations of fabrics will create different effects. The black fabric draws attention to each mola and also acts as a unifying color along the length of the table dressing. Red fabric would create an entirely different look. Border fabrics can echo the bold, bright colors of the molas or stand back in a more pastel background to make sure the molas remain the center of attention.

■ If you don't want to endanger the molas with food stains, make sure the back side is nicely pieced in a pretty design so you can flip both runners over when bringing food to the table. The detail photo shows how the back side of this table dressing is pieced from coordinating fabrics.

Figure 2

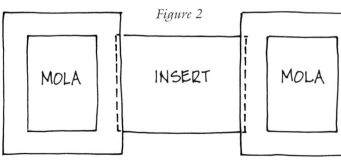

Summer Solstice Pillow

DESIGNER:

Carol McKie Manning

BRIGHTEN UP A WHOLE ROOM with the sizzling colors of summer.
The rich shades and luscious textures of this silk pillow add spectacular drama to an original design.

MATERIALS

- Silk fabrics in the following colors and yardages:

  - ½ yard (.5 m) each of peacock blue, dark violet, purple, red

  - ¼ yard (.25 m) of gold

  - ⅛ yard (.15 m) each of green, blue green, navy blue, dark fuchsia, red orange, light fuchsia, dark purple, soft gold, orange

- Silk fabric of choice for pillow backing

- Threads to match

- Lightweight batting

- Rayon or silk machine embroidery thread in red, gold, and blue

TOOLS & SUPPLIES

- Tracing paper

- Sharp-pointed sewing or embroidery scissors

- Scissors for cutting paper

- Rotary cutter, mat, and ruler

- Pencils and invisible fabric pen

- Roller bobby pins, or other tool for turning under edges

- Iron

- Sewing machine with plastic see-through foot, if available

INSTRUCTIONS

1.

Enlarge Figure 1 to size pillow you would like. The size of the pillow shown here is 17 x 21½" (43 x 54.5 cm), which includes ½" (1.25 cm) seam allowances; finished size is 16 x 20½" (40.5 x 52 cm).

2.

Cut out background in peacock blue, 17 x 21½" (43 x 54.5 cm).

3.

Enlarge and trace the pattern shown in Figure 2 for the dark violet layer, adding ⅛ to ¼" (3 to 6 mm) seam allowances beyond the cutting lines. It helps to color code the patterns you will be making.

4.

Cut out dark violet silk, clipping the curved seam allowances and corners to the foldlines. Turn under the edges along the foldlines, using the tips of your scissors, needle point, or straightened-out bobby pin to urge the edge under.

5.

Lay the dark violet layer over the peacock blue background, pin or baste in place, and sew the folded edges to the layer below with small stitches.

6.

Enlarge and trace the pattern shown in Figure 3 for the purple layer, adding ⅛ to ¼" (3 to 6 mm) seam allowances beyond the cutting lines.

7.

Cut out purple silk, clipping curves and corners to the foldlines. Lay the purple layer over the dark violet, fold the cut edges under, and pin in place. The purple layer will be stitched down after the eye, lip, and sunray inserts are in place.

8.

To make each eye insert, cut a piece of gold silk about 3 x 3" (7.5 x 7.5 cm) or any size that is large enough to hold easily in your hand. Cut out outer dark violet pupil and appliqué to the center of the gold. Cut out inner green pupil and appliqué to the center of the dark violet outer pupil. Trim away the excess gold fabric. Slide inserts under the eyeholes, positioning them so that the eyes appear to look to your right. Stitch folded edges of purple eyeholes to layers below.

9.

Cut out small pieces of fuchsia and blue green for the mouth inserts. Using a fabric pen, mark the foldlines of the purple silk for the mouth detail. Use the sharp-pointed scissors to cut the line for the mouth. Insert the blue green, turn under the purple edges, and stitch down. Do the same for the upper and lower lips, with the fuchsia inserts.

10.

Cut out gold sunray inserts, tracing lines on pattern for purple layer (see Figure 3). Slide under the purple layer, pin or baste in position, and stitch purple folded edges down to layers below.

11.

Make a pattern for the peacock blue upper eyelids. Cut out, clip curves, and stitch to the purple above the eye.

12.

Enlarge and trace the pattern shown in Figure 4 for the red layer. Before cutting out the pattern, lay it over the work-in-progress and make adjustments for any shifting that has occurred.

13.

Cut out red layer, clip curves and corners, and baste on top of purple layer.

14.

For face details, use the fabric pen to mark one at a time. Carefully cut the centers of the designs with sharp-pointed scissors. Clip curves and corners, turn under, and stitch down.

15.

After completing all face details, proceed around sunrays and clip, turn edges under, and stitch down.

For the stem and leaves:

1.

Use your enlargement of Figure 1 to trace a pattern for the flower stem and leaves. Cut out of green fabric.

Figure 1

Figure 2

2.

Using the same pattern, cut shapes slightly smaller out of batting.

3.

Pin or baste stem in position, fold under edges and stitch down one side only.

4.

As you stitch down the other side, use needle point or bobby pin to push batting into stem.

5.

Baste two leaf shapes cut out of green fabric, one at a time, onto larger pieces of blue green and use the fabric pen to mark the spiral design. Clip curved spiral, turn edges under, and stitch down.

6.

Trim away excess blue green background piece to ⅛ to ¼" (3 to 6 mm) inside green leaf edge; clip curves, turn outside edges under, pin in position on pillow, and begin sewing down.

7.

When you are within 1" (2.5 cm) of completion, push batting under the leaf and distribute evenly.

8.

Repeat the process for two more leaves, with green leaf shapes on larger pieces of navy blue.

For the flower:

1.

Use your enlargement of Figure 1 to trace patterns for the flower parts. Cut five petals out of the dark fuchsia and one trumpet shape out of the gold. Using the same pattern, cut shapes slightly smaller out of batting.

2.

Baste petals, one at a time, onto larger pieces of red orange; use fabric pen to mark the inside edge of each petal.

3.

Carefully cut out, clip curves, turn dark fuchsia edges under, and stitch down to red orange.

4.

Baste this two-layer piece onto a larger piece of light fuchsia and use the fabric pen to mark the center design of each petal.

5.

Carefully cut through red orange along

marked lines, clip curves, turn red orange edges under, and stitch down to light fuchsia. Trim away excess background fabrics to ⅛ to ¼" (6 mm) inside petal edges.

6.

Repeat the process with the gold trumpet shape basted onto a larger piece of red orange.

7.

Arrange the flower elements on the pillow and pin in place. Beginning with the petals at the back of the flower and moving forward, sew the appliqué shapes down, pushing batting underneath just before closing them off.

For the hummingbird:

1.

Use your enlargement of Figure 1 to trace seven patterns for the hummingbird—beak, body, two wings, and three tail feathers.

2.

Cut beak out of soft gold and other pieces out of dark purple. Cut shapes slightly smaller out of batting.

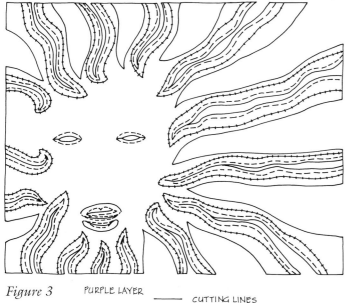

Figure 3   PURPLE LAYER

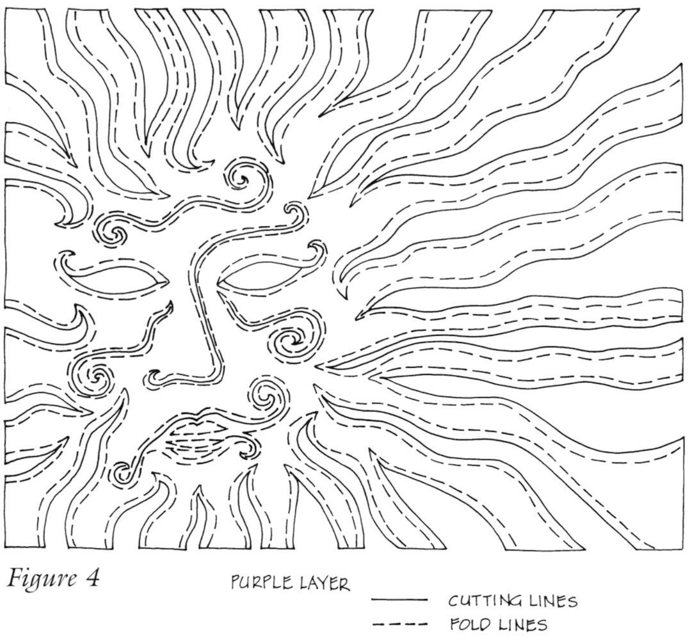

——————— CUTTING LINES
- - - - - FOLD LINES
+++++++ SUNRAY INSERT CUTTING LINES

Figure 4   PURPLE LAYER

——————— CUTTING LINES
- - - - - FOLD LINES

3.

To make eye insert, cut out a piece of green, 5/8 x 1" (1.5 x 2.5 cm). Fold in half lengthwise and sew onto a 2 x 2" (5 x 5 cm) piece of gold fabric. Use the fabric pen to mark the eyehole on the hummingbird's body shape; slit it open and turn the edges under. Slide the eye insert into position and stitch down the eyehole edges. Trim away the gold background.

4.

Baste the body shape onto a larger piece of dark fuchsia. Mark designs with fabric pen, carefully cut out, clip curves and corners, turn dark purple edges under, and stitch down to dark fuchsia.

5.

Baste this piece onto a piece of orange. Mark design, cut open, turn dark fuchsia edges under, and sew down to orange.

6.

Repeat process for other bird body parts, changing the under-layer colors as desired.

7.

Arrange bird body appliqué shapes on the pillow and pin in place. Beginning with the back tail feather and moving forward, sew the feather shapes down, pushing batting underneath just before closing them off. Repeat with the back wing, then the body, the front wing, and finally, the beak.

To finish pillow:

1.

Cut a piece of batting, 17 x 21½" (43 x 54.5 cm). Place under the completed pillow face and pin in place. Machine stitch all around, 3/8" (1 cm) from the edge.

2.

With rayon or silk thread, machine quilt through all layers, using the appliqué design to suggest stitching lines. You may want to mark the stitching lines with the fabric pen before starting. Begin quilting with the face area, and continue out into the sunrays and sky. Do not stitch over the flower and hummingbird designs.

3.

Cut a piece of backing fabric and a piece of batting, 17 x 21½" (43 x 54.5 cm). Pin them together and machine sew around the edges. Draw a loose quilting design on the backing fabric and machine quilt the layers together.

4.

With right sides facing, stitch pillow front and back together, using ½" (1.25 cm) seam allowances and leaving an opening of about 6" (15 cm) at the bottom.

5.

Clip corners and turn pillow right side out through opening. Stuff pillow and hand stitch opening shut.

TIPS

■ Improvise a handy tool for getting the edges to turn under by straightening out a large roller bobby pin and removing the rubber tip. The wavy part makes it easier to grip while folding under the seam allowance.

■ Silk fabric gives a glowing sheen to this sunny pattern—a perfect marriage of design and fabric. However, experimenting with different materials will give you varying effects.

Mola Spirit Dolls

DESIGNER:

Lynne Sward

DESIGN SOME CUSTOM MOLA FABRICS and then transform them completely into these three-dimensional spirit dolls.
Add some wild hair, dress them up in colorful clothes, and give them special names like these—
Not Barbie Doll, Southwest Spirit, and Reggae Spirit.

MATERIALS

- Geometric design from copyright-free clip art book

- ½ yard (.5 m) each of two coordinating or contrasting cotton fabrics for each doll, for top and bottom layers

- Fusible woven interfacing

- Double-face fusible stabilizer

- Plain and variegated thread to match or coordinate with fabrics

- Assorted scraps of cotton fabrics, Ultrasuede, rickrack, yarn

- Polyester fiberfill stuffing

TOOLS & SUPPLIES

- Sharp-point scissors, rotary cutter, or craft knife

- Scissors for cutting paper

- Plain paper

- Sewing machine

- Wooden chopstick

INSTRUCTIONS

1.

Select a geometric or linear design that has a "mola" look from clip art book and make a photocopy of it. Photocopy the copy at an enlarged size, and do this three more times until the final design is large and the elements are spread out enough to be cut out of fabric. See Figure 1.

2.

Make two large-size copies, 11 x 17" (28 x 43 cm), of the final enlargement so you will have enough of a design to construct the mola fabric for the doll pattern.

3.

Cut out the black background areas of the paper design, using sharp paper-cutting scissors or a craft knife. You don't have to cut out each and every black shape; you can skip areas for visual effect.

4.

Select the top layer fabric for each doll and iron fusible stabilizer to the wrong side.

5.

Pin enlarged cut-out paper patterns on right side and, with sharp-point scissors or rotary cutter, cut the fabric out of the open areas. Try to make clean and straight cutting lines.

6.

Remove paper patterns. Peel paper backing off stabilizer and fuse the cut fabric onto the selected bottom background fabric.

7.

Set sewing machine to a narrow and slightly shortened zigzag stitch. Choose a matching, contrasting, or variegated thread and zigzag around all the raw cut-out edges of the top mola layer. Pull threads to back side and trim or tie off.

8.

On plain paper, draw the outline of the doll's body shape and cut out, to make a "viewing window."

9.

Place viewing window on top of the layered and stitched mola fabric and move it around until you see a pattern arrangement that you want to show. This is where you will place the body pattern piece and cut it out for the front of the doll. See Figure 2.

10.

For the back of the doll, cut another doll body shape from the unstitched

background fabric. Layer fused fabric shapes left over from the front fabric onto background fabric as desired and sew with zigzag stitch.

11.

Fuse interfacing to wrong side of doll front and back.

12.

With right sides facing, stitch doll front to back, ¼" (6 mm) from edge, leaving neck open. Clip curves and turn doll to right side.

13.

Stuff doll firmly with polyester fiberfill, using the chopstick to push stuffing into place. Stuff to the first dotted line, at the top of the legs, as shown on the doll pattern. Machine stitch across this line and continue stuffing. Treat hands and arms the same way, stitching across the wrist and underarm indicated on the doll pattern.

14.

To make the face, choose a head shape and cut out twice. With right sides facing, stitch ¼" (6 mm) around edge, leaving a small opening. Turn to right side through opening, and hand stitch closed. Iron stabilizer to back side of assorted fabric scraps, cut out small face details, remove paper backing, and fuse to front of face. Repeat for back of head.

Figure 1

Copy 1

Copy 2

Copy 3

Copy 4

Copy 5

Doll Heads

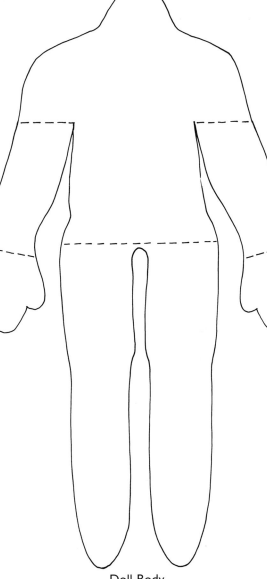

Figure 2

Doll Body

15.

To make the hair, hand sew assorted fabric strips, Ultrasuede strips, rickrack, and yarn to a scrap of fabric. Insert fabric scrap into neck opening and hand stitch neck closed.

16.

Blind-stitch face and back of head to front and back of doll. Slip stitch face and back of head to each other around outside edge.

17.

The clothes on Not Barbie Doll are made from Ultrasuede. Iron stabilizer to wrong side, cut designs out freehand, peel away paper backing, and fuse Ultrasuede to a piece of background fabric. Zigzag or hand overcast around cut-out designs and hand stitch clothes to doll.

TIPS

■ The new shaped-edge scissors cut interesting textures, such as scallops and wavy lines. You can also use regular scissors, or tear strips by hand for a frizzy hair look.

■ If your dolls are for display, rather than play, tack a small loop of yarn or rickrack on the back of each one, for hanging on the wall.

Mola Tote Bag

DESIGNER:

Jan N. Hildebrand

START WITH YOUR FAVORITE TOTE BAG PATTERN and then make it one-of-a-kind with this mola-inspired design. Ideas can come from anywhere—the cat image on this tote, taken from a cast-iron door stop, is supposed to ward off evil spirits.

MATERIALS

- Fabric for tote bag
- Contrasting fabric, cut to 12 x 12" (30.5 x 30.5 cm) square
- Scraps of coordinating fabrics
- Matching and contrasting thread
- Fusible web product

TOOLS AND SUPPLIES

- Sewing machine with decorative stitch options
- Freezer paper
- Iron
- Scissors, pins, pencil

INSTRUCTIONS

1.

Assemble the tote bag, according to pattern instructions, far enough along that the area for the mola design is ready.

2.

Cut a 12 x 12" (30.5 x 30.5 cm) square of freezer paper. Enlarge and draw the main cat design on it.

3.

Layer the freezer paper on top (waxy side down), then the contrasting fabric square, and then the fusible web.

4.

Iron the freezer paper side, to temporarily stick the design to the fabric so you can cut it out and to bond the fusible web to the back of the fabric so it will stick to the tote bag.

5.

Cut out the main cat design, cutting along the lines drawn on the freezer paper. Trim the cat design about ¼" (6 mm) all around; pull the paper backing

off and fuse the cat to the tote.

6.

Cut the other designs out of what's left of the fabric square.

7.

Tuck scraps of coordinating fabrics behind the cutouts, pin in place, and fuse the remaining fabric square to the tote.

8.

Using matching or contrasting thread, depending on the effect you want, machine stitch all raw edges with a blanket stitch.

9.

Add a frame around the mola square, using contrasting fabric strips with edges folded under or bias strips.

10.

Decorate the frame with a machine embroidery stitch of your choice.

11.

Complete and line the tote bag, according to pattern instructions.

TIPS

- Depending on the pattern you use, you can either partially assemble the tote first or wait until after you have added the mola panel to the front piece.

- Turn the tote bag into a showcase for your creative hand embroidery or beadwork, adding these embellishments after the mola design is complete.

Two Berets and Tote Bag

DESIGNER:

Mary Russell

TOP OFF YOUR OUTFIT with some bright mola accessories like these nifty berets and a handy tote bag. Easy to make, quick to stitch, you can whip them up in a jiffy and head out the door.

MATERIALS

- ½ yard (.5 m) of 45" (115 cm) wool and lining fabric for each beret
- ½ yard (.5 m) of 45" (115 cm) wool and lining fabric for tote bag
- Medium-weight fusible interfacing
- Matching thread
- Rayon machine embroidery thread in assorted colors of choice
- Stabilizer or newsprint

TOOLS & SUPPLIES

- Pencil or fabric marker
- Scissors
- Sewing machine
- Appliqué, open-toe, or see-through sewing machine foot, if available
- Iron
- Terrycloth towel and pressing cloth
- Plastic needlepoint canvas for tote bag
- Two bracelets or large rings for handles, 4" (10 cm) in diameter, for tote bag

INSTRUCTIONS

Loosen upper tension on sewing machine and set for a wide satin stitch, with thread to match fabric in bobbin and rayon machine embroidery thread on top. An appliqué, open-toe, or see-through sewing machine foot is recommended for satin stitching the designs.

For the beret:

1.

Following the pattern, cut out band for beret. The band is 2½" (6.5 cm) wide, including ½" (1.25 cm) seam allowances. The band is 22½" (57 cm) long for a small size, 24" (61 cm) for a medium size, and 25" (63.5 cm) for a large size.

2.

Cut band interfacing and fuse to the wrong size of the band, following manufacturer's instructions.

3.

With a pencil, trace the brim and crown pattern pieces onto stabilizer or newsprint. Cut the stabilizer 1" (2.5 cm) larger than the pattern for each piece. Pin the stabilizer pattern to the right side of the fabric and cut fabric just outside of the stabilizer.

4.

Using a wide satin stitch and selected thread colors, sew through the stabilizer and fabric along the penciled design lines. Tie off thread at the start and finish of each line, and change thread colors as desired.

5.

For triple line of stitching on brim, sew one row of wide satin stitch and then another row adjacent to it; do not overlap the stitches. Switch to a medium satin stitch and another color of thread, and overlay a third row of stitching along the center line of the previous two rows.

6.

Proceed to stitch penciled designs on brim and crown. Pivot when necessary to keep stitches perpendicular to the outline. Overlay the wide fish backbones with a narrow satin stitch down the middle.

7.

To fill in the outline for the eyes, vary the stitch width as you go. Start with a narrow width at one end, widen it as you approach the center, and narrow as you approach the other end. Another option is to use a programmable machine's circular stitch.

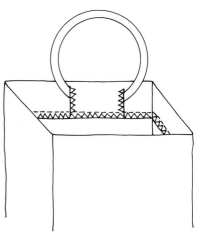

Figure 1

PATTERN FOR TOTE BAG

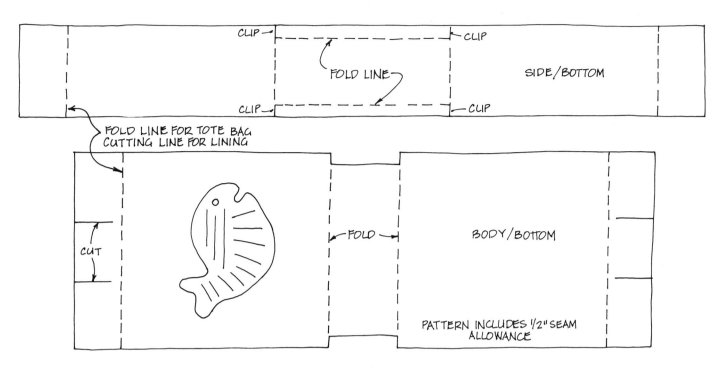

CLIP → ← CLIP

FOLD LINE →

SIDE/BOTTOM

CLIP → ← CLIP

FOLD LINE FOR TOTE BAG
CUTTING LINE FOR LINING

CUT

← FOLD →

BODY/BOTTOM

PATTERN INCLUDES ½" SEAM ALLOWANCE

8.

Remove the stabilizer. Press the brim and crown by placing on the terrycloth towel with stitching toward the towel. Steam gently from the back, using a pressing cloth. Let the fabric cool on the towel, and move it only when it is cool and dry.

9.

Pin pattern pieces to fabric, matching the satin stitch designs with the pattern outlines, and trim the brim and crown pieces to actual size.

10.

Change sewing machine tension back to normal before assembling beret and switch to straight stitch foot.

11.

With right sides facing, stitch brim and crown together with ½" (1.25 cm) seam allowances. Press seam open. From the right side, topstitch on both sides of the seamline to hold allowances in place.

12.

For the lining, cut a brim and crown, and assemble as you did the beret. Press the seam toward the crown.

13.

With wrong sides facing, sew lining to beret ¼" (6 mm) away from opening edge with a long straight stay stitch.

14.

Stitch the ends of the band together; press seam open. Pin band to the beret opening with right sides together and stitch in a ½" (1.25 cm) seam.

15.

Trim seam allowance to ¼" (6 mm) and clip every ½" (1.25 cm). Press seam toward brim. Finish raw edge of band with a zigzag stitch and fold band in half to inside of the beret so the finished edge covers the seam.

16.

From the right side, stitch through the seam allowance to hold the band in place. Press band flat.

For the tote bag:

1.

Enlarge and trace the body/bottom pattern piece onto stabilizer. Cut the stabilizer 1" (2.5 cm) larger all around the pattern. Pin the stabilizer pattern to the right side of the fabric and cut the fabric just outside of the stabilizer.

2.

Cut the side/bottom piece out of the fabric to actual size.

3.

Using the same settings you did for the beret, stitch the fish designs through the stabilizer and fabric.

4.

Remove the stabilizer and press on the terrycloth towel, as above. Let cool completely before moving.

5.

Pin pattern pieces to fabric and trim the bag body/bottom to actual size.

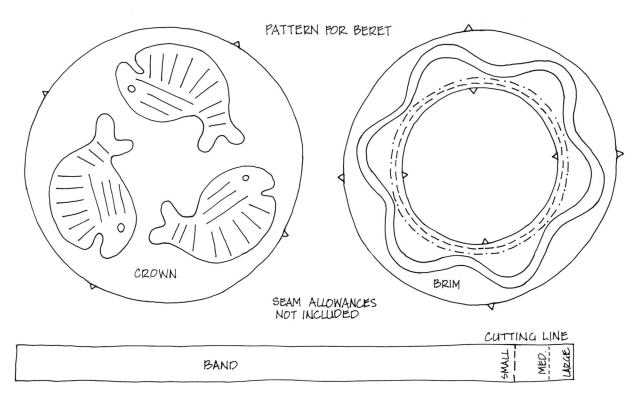

PATTERN FOR BERET

CROWN

BRIM

SEAM ALLOWANCES
NOT INCLUDED

BAND

CUTTING LINE

SMALL   MED.   LARGE

6.

Interface the shorter edges of the body/bottom and side/bottom with 3" (7.5 cm) strips of interfacing. These edges will become the top of the tote bag.

7.

Clip the side/bottom to seamline where indicated on the pattern. Turn the seam allowance under between the clips and press.

8.

With right sides up, place the side/bottom piece over the body/bottom piece so they are perpendicular to each other. The pieces will form a cross or plus sign and the notched-out places will overlap. Stitch the bottom of the bag along three sides, close to the edge.

9.

Cut two pieces of plastic needlepoint canvas, 7 x 2⅝" (18 x 6.75 cm), and insert them into the pocket formed at the bottom of the bag.

10.

Change to a zipper foot for this step only and stitch the fourth side.

11.

Fold bag sides up and stitch right sides together with a ½" (1.25 cm) seam allowance, widening to a ⅝" (1.5 cm) seam at the bottom of the bag. Press each seam open after stitching.

12.

Finish the upper raw edge of the bag with a zigzag stitch. Slash along guidelines to ⅜" (1 cm) from seamline, so handles can be inserted. See Figure 1.

13.

Cut lining to the actual pattern size. Note that the cutting line for the lining is the foldline for the top of the bag. Stitch lining together as you did the bag, omitting the insertion of plastic canvas in bottom.

14.

Turn bag right side out and fold top edge under 2" (5 cm). Place lining inside bag so the top edge of the lining fits inside the folded edge of the bag. Pin in place.

15.

Topstitch around the top of the bag, ⅜" (1 cm) from the edge.

16.

Slip a bracelet under each flap and stitch folded edge in place.

TIPS

■ Make up some samples of narrow, medium, and wide satin stitches on your selected fabric to see how it covers and to get used to pivoting while sewing curves and angles. You'll be a master at it when it's time to make the beret and tote bag.

■ Instead of using bangle bracelets for the bag handles, sew some matching or contrasting bands and decorate them with mola-inspired stitching before attaching to the bag.

The designer wishes to thank Sulky of America for the rayon thread used in this project.

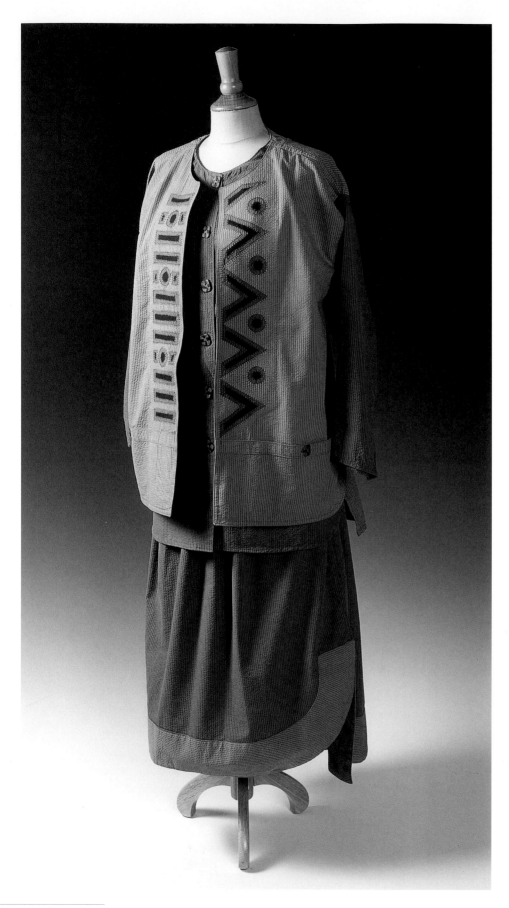

Tunic and Skirt Ensemble

DESIGNER:

Lori Kerr

A STANDARD SEWING PATTERN for a skirt and coordinating overblouse will stand out from the crowd when special features are added to it. Here, a reverse appliqué mola design down the front of an attached faux vest and a shaped skirt hemline with contrasting reverse facings make this outfit extraordinary.

MATERIALS

- Pattern for full skirt

- Pattern for tunic or overblouse

- Assorted contrasting or coordinating fabrics for skirt, blouse, vest fronts, vest front lining, skirt facings, and reverse appliqué layers

- Double-faced fusible stabilizer

- Matching and contrasting threads

TOOLS & SUPPLIES

- Sewing machine

- Sharp-pointed scissors

- Pencil or chalk

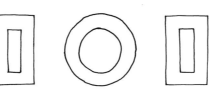

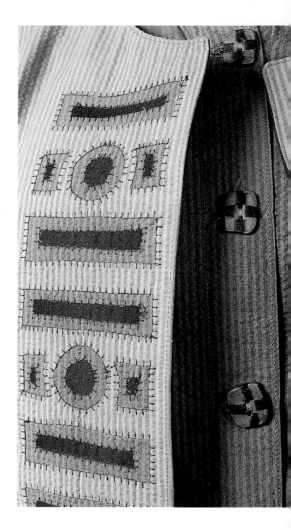

INSTRUCTIONS

1.

Cut out skirt and blouse pieces. For the skirt's shaped hem, curve the front cutting line at the side seams, using a dinner plate or other round object as a guide.

2.

For vest fronts, trace the blouse pattern's front pieces, but make the hem shorter and cut the front of the armhole about $\frac{1}{4}$" (6 mm) larger. Also, lower the front neckline about $\frac{1}{4}$" (6 mm), tapering to zero at the shoulder. You may wish to shape the vest neckline in other ways—scalloped or V-neck, for instance.

3.

Cut a strip of stabilizer long enough and wide enough for each column of mola motifs and iron to the wrong side of each vest front. Transfer the outer lines of each mola pattern onto the stabilizer with pencil or chalk.

4.

Cut the design out of both stabilizer and vest front fabric.

5.

Peel backing away and fuse to the selected middle layer fabric.

6.

Iron strips of stabilizer to the back of the middle layer over the areas that will be cut. Transfer the inner lines of each mola pattern onto the stabilizer, cut out, peel backing away, and fuse to pieces of the bottom layer fabric.

7.

On the right side, blanket-stitch the raw edges around each cut-out area, using rayon embroidery thread.

8.

Assemble and line vest fronts, disregarding pattern instructions regarding back. The fabric used to line the vest fronts shown here is the same purple cotton as the bottom layer of the mola design.

9.

Assemble blouse, remembering to stitch vest fronts into shoulder and side seams.

10.

Assemble skirt, stopping side seam stitching where curved front hemline begins.

11.

Finish skirt hem with contrast reverse facings. Use the bottom edges of the skirt pattern as a guide to cut bands of contrasting material as wide as desired.

With right side of band facing wrong side of skirt, stitch along hemline and side seams. Press seam toward band. Turn band to outside, so right side will show. Turn under raw edge and edgestitch to skirt.

TIPS

■ There are so many options for combining fabrics in this outfit. The blouse shown here uses olive fabric for the sleeves and front pieces; the back piece is cut from the same light brown fabric as the attached faux vest fronts. The result creates the illusion of an entire light brown vest worn over an olive blouse.

Vest with Mola Pockets

DESIGNER:

Charlotte Patera

SHARPEN YOUR MOLA-MAKING SKILLS with these square panels and then use them to turn a simple vest into something special. Their bright colors could also emblazon a jacket, pillows, or a tote bag.

MATERIALS

- Six blocks of fabric, 9 x 9½" (23 x 24 cm), in the following colors:

- one each in hot pink and turquoise, for the middle layers

- two in black, for the foundation layers

- two dark red, for the top layer

- Assorted fabric scraps in coordinated bright colors and dark colors

- Thread to match all colors

TOOLS AND SUPPLIES

- Dressmaker's tracing carbon paper or other transfer tools

- Sharp-pointed embroidery scissors

- Needles (size 10 Milliner's Straw needle, size 10 Embroidery needle, or size 10, 11, or 12 Sharp)

INSTRUCTIONS

1.

Trace the bird pattern to one of the middle layers of hot pink or turquoise, centering it on the panel to allow for ample allowance all around. See Figure 1.

2.

Pin the two middle layers together and use the sharp point of your scissors to pierce the fabric and cut along the traced line, being careful not to cut outside the line. See Figure 2.

3.

Separate the two birds from the two surrounding backgrounds. See Figure 3.

4.

Position these four pieces onto the black foundation panels and pin in place, swapping the birds so the pink one is on top of the turquoise background, and the turquoise is on the pink. Reverse the position of one of the panels, by flipping the cut fabrics over, so the birds face each other. See Figure 4.

5.

Sew each background piece to its panel by folding under the inside edge about ⅛" (3 mm) and stitching it invisibly. This will form an outline around the center bird shape. Work along the edge a little bit at a time, clipping the fabric as needed to turn it under (see Figure 5 on page 42 about stitching inside curves). See Figure 5.

6.

Sew each bird piece to its panel by folding under the outside edge about ⅛" (3 mm) and stitching it invisibly. This will widen the outline around the bird to about ¼" (6 mm) to reveal the black foundation layer. See Figure 5. Work along the edge a little bit at a time, notching the fabric as needed to turn it under (see Figure 6 on page 42 about stitching outside curves).

NOTE: You now have two simple three-color molas. You can stop at this point, embellish the mola panels with beads for bird eyes, and incorporate them into another project. Or, you can continue by adding the red fabric layer and the additional appliqué shapes in other colors.

© 1985 Charlotte Patera

Figure 1

⅛" (3 mm), and stitch on top of their matching shapes on the bird. See Figure 9. The turned-under edges of these shapes are indicated by the dashed lines in Figure 1, and when stitched, will reveal an outline of the layer below.

14.

For the appliqué over the feathers, cut one piece of dark fabric to cover the whole group. Position the piece over the feathers and feel the stitched edges underneath, as you did when stitching the red layer over the hidden bird. Begin by folding under and stitching the upper edge, to cover the tops of the feathers. Then, fold under one edge along the first feather to reveal about ⅛" (3 mm) of the feather shape below, and stitch down. See Figure 9. Work a little bit at a time; do not attempt to cut all the feathers at once. For details about stitching inside and outside corners, see page 41.

15.

The remaining open space will be filled with slits of inlaid appliqué (see page 36 for details about this technique). Mark the vertical slits onto the top layer, according to the pattern in Figure 1. You may wish to make fewer slits than the pattern shows. Divide the slits into groups and cut a piece of contrasting fabric to fit underneath each group.

16.

Insert each fabric piece under the top layer of fabric and baste or pin in place. See Figure 10 for how to inlay the pieces. Note that the smaller inlay piece will be inserted through the larger slit and spread out underneath both slits.

17.

Cut along each slit line, clipping a Y-cut at the top and bottom. Fold under the edges of each slit and stitch them down. See Figure 11.

7.

Pin a piece of the red fabric on top of each panel. The bird image is now completely covered. See Figure 6.

8.

You will need to cut through the red layer around the bird outline on each panel, even though it is not visible. By running your fingernail or a sharp pencil around the edges of the bird, you will be able to feel the ridges created by the stitched edges underneath and can trace them. Unpin the red layer and peek underneath, as needed.

9.

Starting with the outside edge, cut along the traced line a little bit at a time, fold it under, and stitch in place. Try to keep the newly folded edge an even distance from the stitched-down edge of the layer below. Repeat with the inside edge. See Figure 7.

10.

Trace the bird feathers onto fabric scraps of bright colors, following the solid lines in Figure 1. The feathers and other details will be added to the mola panels with overlay appliqué (see page 36 for details about this technique).

11.

Cut the feather shapes, adding a ⅛" (3 mm) turn-under allowance. Place them on the bird according to the pattern in Figure 1, fold under the edges, and stitch down. See Figure 8.

12.

Repeat for the eye and the leaves, tracing along the solid lines and adding a ⅛" (3 mm) turn-under allowance.

13.

Trace along the solid lines of the pattern for the eye and leaves, but do not add a turn-under allowance. Cut these out of the dark colors, turn under the edges

18.

For the dots on the leaves, make a small Y-cut, fold under the edges, and stitch. See Figure 12.

19.

Add optional chain-stitch embroidery to the birds' heads, as desired.

20.

Assemble a simple vest pattern that has a straight, square-cut front hem.

21.

Line the mola panels, using a ½" (1.25 cm) seam allowance all around.

22.

Stitch the mola panels to the vest fronts, leaving side edges unsewn, to form pocket openings.

Figure 3

Figure 2

KEY TO FABRICS:

▢ PINK

▨ TURQUOISE

TIPS

■ A traditional mola has nearly every bit of "blank" space worked, and slits are one of the common ways to do this. In these mola panels, you inlay or insert small scraps of fabric behind the slits to add even more colors. However, if you do not add these fabrics, you will save a step and the slits will be the color of the middle layer, which may be colorful enough for you.

■ You can omit several steps of these molas, depending on your appliqué skills or patience. You can stop after step #6, #13, #14, or #17 and still have two beautiful panels with that "mola" feeling.

Figure 4

KEY TO FABRICS:

▢ PINK

▨ TURQUOISE

■ BLACK

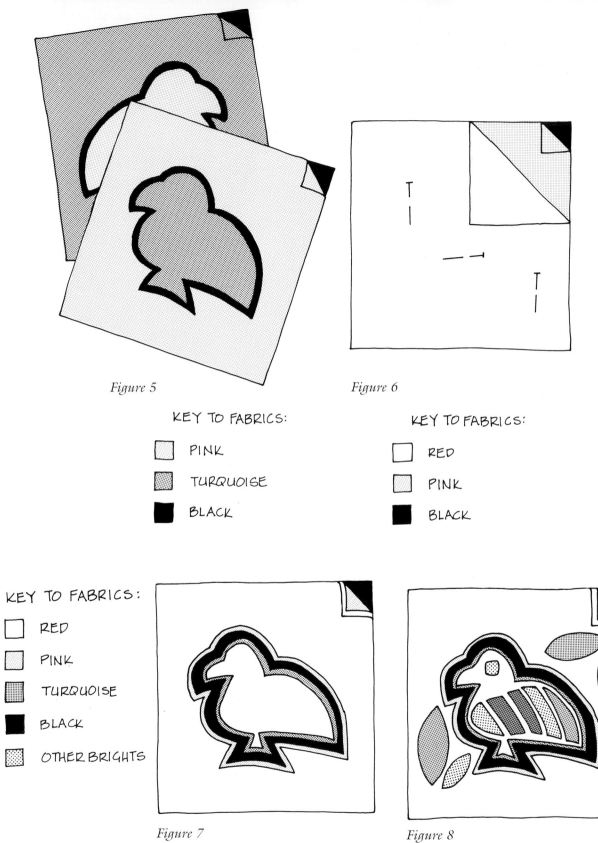

Figure 5

Figure 6

KEY TO FABRICS:

⬜ PINK

▨ TURQUOISE

⬛ BLACK

KEY TO FABRICS:

⬜ RED

▨ PINK

⬛ BLACK

KEY TO FABRICS:

⬜ RED

⬜ PINK

▨ TURQUOISE

⬛ BLACK

▨ OTHER BRIGHTS

Figure 7

Figure 8

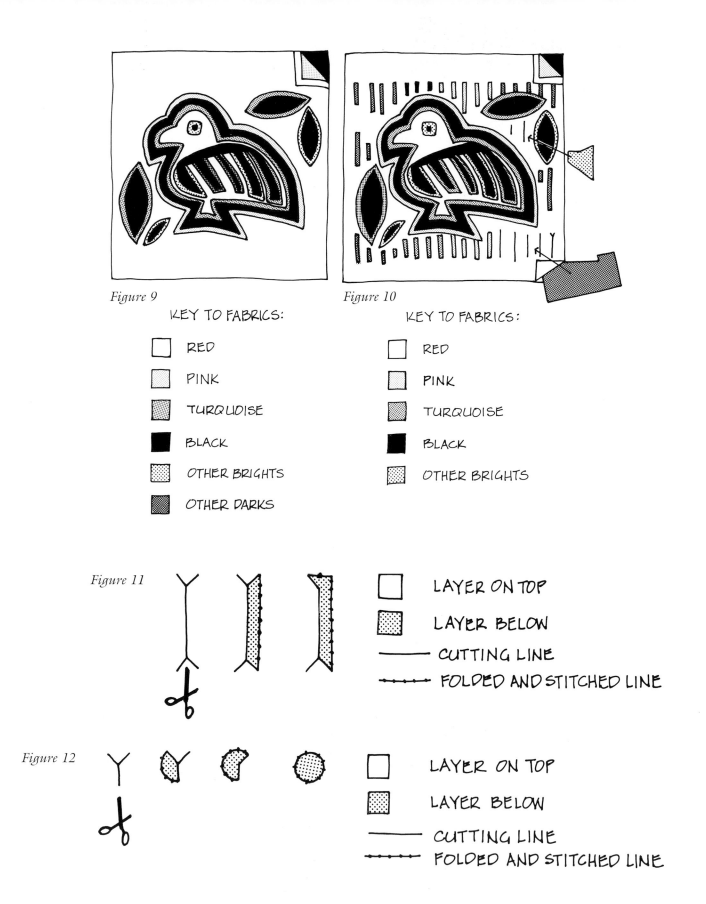

Figure 9

KEY TO FABRICS:

☐ RED

▨ PINK

▨ TURQUOISE

■ BLACK

▨ OTHER BRIGHTS

▨ OTHER DARKS

Figure 10

KEY TO FABRICS:

☐ RED

▨ PINK

▨ TURQUOISE

■ BLACK

▨ OTHER BRIGHTS

Figure 11

☐ LAYER ON TOP

▨ LAYER BELOW

— CUTTING LINE

•••• FOLDED AND STITCHED LINE

Figure 12

☐ LAYER ON TOP

▨ LAYER BELOW

— CUTTING LINE

•••• FOLDED AND STITCHED LINE

Four Geckos Vest

DESIGNER:

Virginia J. Schlosser

WRAP YOURSELF UP in your favorite design, inside and out, like this exciting vest inspired by traditional molas and the markings of gecko lizards.

MATERIALS

- Pattern for vest without darts
- Selected design, enlarged to desired size
- Black, red, and yellow fabrics, enough for vest fronts and back
- Lining fabric for vest fronts and back
- Fusible interfacing for front edge and back neckline
- Double-faced fusible stabilizer
- Rayon machine embroidery thread to match

TOOLS AND SUPPLIES

- Heavyweight paper, to glue design to
- Rubber cement or glue
- Chalk pencil and ruler
- Scissors for cutting fabric and paper
- Plain paper
- Sewing machine
- Iron

INSTRUCTIONS

1.

Cut vest fronts and back out of the three layers of fabric. You will cut the lining pieces later.

2.

Trace the design onto heavyweight paper, glue in place, and cut out. Determine where you want the main design to be by moving the paper pattern around on the vest until you get a placement you like. The vest shown here has one gecko on each front and two on the back.

3.

Iron stabilizer to the wrong side of the black top layer fabric. Draw or trace the design on the paper backing in reverse, so that it will be facing the way you

want on the right side of the fabric. Cut out the design through the paper and the black fabric.

4.

Remove the paper backing and fuse the black layer to the middle red layer.

5.

With black rayon embroidery thread in the needle, satin stitch around the cut edges of the design, tapering in the corners and at points.

6.

Iron stabilizer to the wrong side of the red fabric behind the design. Draw or transfer the lines on the body of each gecko. Cut out the design, remove the paper backing, and place on the yellow bottom layer of fabric. Check placement of the lines and fuse in place.

7.

With red rayon thread in the needle, satin stitch around the cut edges of the design, tapering in the corners and at points.

8.

Baste three fabric layers together around armhole and outside edges.

9.

Use a chalk pencil and ruler to mark the straight slash lines on the black background. Use random distances between the lines and don't make them all the same length.

10.

With yellow rayon thread in the needle, satin stitch over the chalked lines to complete the overall design. Gently press each vest section on the wrong side.

11.

Cut out lining for vest fronts and back.

12.

Select one of the geckos you cut out of the top layer and pin in desired position on right side of back lining piece. Satin stitch around the edges.

13.

Cut out interfacing for the front edges and back neckline, and fuse to wrong side of lining. Depending on the fabric you have chosen, you may want to fuse interfacing to both front pieces to stiffen them.

14.

Assemble vest and attach decorative closures, such as buttons or frogs.

TIPS

■ Don't forget to preshrink all fabrics before starting, including interfacings, even if the finished vest will be dry cleaned. This will prevent any puckering, shifting, or shrinking later on.

■ The options for the front closing are many. Use unique buttons as a purely ornamental addition, attach appliquéd tie ends, or look for a dramatic clasp.

Chenille Lizard Vest

DESIGNER:

Sandy Webster

A MOCK CHENILLE TECHNIQUE with wide-cut channels in the top layer add up to a bold and fun vest for a creative variation on the mola theme. Line the vest with an ethnic print fabric for super design interest. The lizard design on the back of this vest was inspired by an old South American clay stamp.

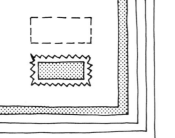

Figure 1

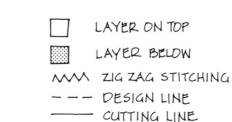

LAYER ON TOP

LAYER BELOW

ZIG ZAG STITCHING

DESIGN LINE

CUTTING LINE

MATERIALS

- Vest pattern of choice

- Enough machine washable material to make five layers of the vest in coordinating or contrasting solids

- Lining fabric of choice

- Fabric for wide bias trim for all edges

TOOLS & SUPPLIES

- Sewing machine
- Sharp-pointed scissors
- Washable ink marking pen

INSTRUCTIONS

1.

Cut vest pattern out of all five fabrics, but do not assemble; layer the fabrics in the order you wish them to appear when cut, and pin together carefully.

2.

With washable ink marker, draw the desired pattern on the top layer. Keep the design lines far enough apart so that the layers of fabric will be nicely exposed when the space inside the lines is cut away. See Figure 1.

3.

Reduce both the stitch length and width of your sewing machine's zigzag setting so it's almost a satin stitch, and sew along the design lines.

4.

When all lines have been covered with stitching, trim away as many layers of fabric as you desire, choosing which color or layer you want to be visible in any area. Trim close to the stitching line.

5.

Cut the vest pattern pieces out of the lining fabric and place them on the bottom of their matching five-layer fabric stacks.

6.

Sew the vest pieces together at the shoulders and side seams, with seam allowances to the outside.

7.

Wash and dry vest several times to loosen threads from the cut edges; trim loosened threads after each washing.

The result of all the washing and drying should resemble chenille.

8.

Cut bias strips about 1½" (4 cm) wide and machine stitch to the armhole and outside edges of the vest; turn strips to inside and hand stitch in place.

9.

Wash vest one more time and trim any loose ends.

TIPS

- Use loosely woven washable cottons because they will easily fray in the wash. Also, because fabric frays more along the straight of grain than the bias, plan your designs to take advantage of lines along the crosswise or lengthwise grain. When you cut along them, threads will loosen easily.

- Purchase bedspreads and tablecloths from import stores for the lining and edging. They are large pieces, which makes it easy to cut bias strips from them, and they complement the ethnic quality of mola-inspired designs.

Tivoli Jacket
DESIGNER:
Faye Anderson

HERE'S A DAZZLING VARIATION on a mola theme. Start with a favorite pattern, cut out windows that reveal brilliant patterns below, and top off the high-color creation with decorative stitching and an exuberant fringe of fabric tubes.

MATERIALS

- Pattern for basic no-lapel jacket or vest with few, if any, darts

- Yardage, as required by pattern, in a solid color (material should have an even, tight weave with little texture)

- White, lightweight to medium-weight fusible interfacing, equal to yardage required for jacket or vest

- Assorted small pieces of bright solid-colored and print cotton fabrics

- Thread to match main fabric

- Contrasting decorative thread, such as topstitching, variegated, rayon, or metallic

- Sheer nylon bias seam finishing tape, 1¼" (3 cm) wide

- ½ yard (.5 m) bright cotton print for tube fringe

- Jacket lining fabric of choice

TOOLS & SUPPLIES

- Rotary cutter, mat, and ruler
- Sewing machine
- Iron
- Small, sharp-pointed scissors
- Bias tube maker
- Permanent marking pen

INSTRUCTIONS

1.
Cut jacket out of fashion fabric.

2.
Cut jacket out of fusible interfacing; trim off seam allowances.

3.
Calculate an on-grain grid that will cover your pattern pieces evenly (this varies with each pattern style and size). For example, a 3" (7.5 cm) grid was

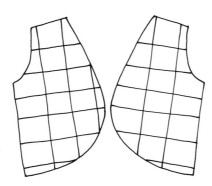 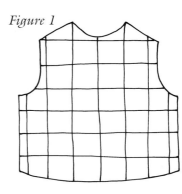

Figure 1

used for the jacket shown here, but a 3½" (9 cm) or 4" (10 cm) grid might work better for your pattern. Do not include the seam allowance areas in the calculation. This grid will form the windowpane that you will fill with squares of contrasting fabric. See Figure 1.
NOTE: Because the pattern pieces are not squares, there will be many odd-shaped slivers left over in the windowpane grid.

4.
Use the permanent marker to draw the grid on the adhesive side of the interfacing pieces.

5.
Cut squares of contrasting fabrics the same size as your grid and as many as you need to fill the grid. To speed the process, use a rotary cutter, ruler, and mat.

6.
Place one interfacing piece adhesive side up on the ironing board; position contrasting squares, right sides up, on the grid in an arrangement that you like. When all the full grid squares are covered, fill in any exposed adhesive sections with little bits of fabric. All of the adhesive must be covered. See Figure 2.

7.
With a damp pressing cloth, fuse all the contrasting squares to the interfacing, according to the manufacturer's instructions. Repeat with remaining jacket front or back sections.

8.
Lay each front and back fashion fabric piece, right side down, and cover with their matching interfacing pieces, contrasting squares down. Hand baste around outside edges and along grid lines, to keep layers from shifting.

Figure 2

Figure 3
Back

Figure 4

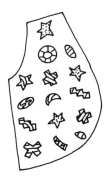

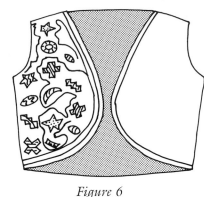

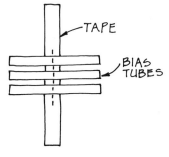

Figure 5

Front

Figure 6

Figure 7

Figure 8

Stitching around
shapes

Figure 9

TAPE

BIAS
TUBES

9.

Draw a simple, stylized shape in each full square of the interfacing grid. See Figure 3. Leave 1/4" (6 mm) margin around each design. Use shapes of your choice, including hearts, circles, crosses, bold zigzags, stars, etc. See Figure 4 for ideas.

10.

Using a very short stitch length, carefully machine stitch around each shape, working from the back. Lift the presser foot frequently, shifting the fabric to follow the marked design lines.

11.

With very sharp scissors, carefully cut away each shape from the top fashion fabric layer, approximately 1/8" (3 mm) from the stitched lines. Take care not to cut through more than the top layer. The lower layer of contrasting fabric is now revealed, in mola-like fashion. See Figure 5. Satin stitch raw edges of the shapes, if you desire a more polished look.

12.

Stitch darts, side and shoulder seams, and press.

13.

With a contrasting decorative thread, stitch around all shapes, meandering from one to another. Topstitch three rows, 1/4" (6 mm) apart, around the outside edge. See Figure 6.

14.

For the sleeves, place a row of contrasting squares along the lower edge of the sleeve interfacing (adhesive side) and fuse this area. See Figure 7.

15.

Lay fashion fabric sleeve on top, wrong side down, and fuse remaining area of sleeve. Although only the lower edge of the sleeve has mola cutwork, the entire piece needs to be interfaced to have the same body as the rest of the garment.

16.

Hand baste around outside edges and color blocks, draw shapes on back of interfacing, and stitch and cut as you did on jacket front and back sections in steps #10 and 11.

17.

With decorative thread, machine stitch, as you did in step #13, around the shapes and in a meandering fashion on the remaining part of the sleeve. See Figure 8.

18.

Sew the under sleeve seam and insert sleeves in jacket.

19.

For the fringe, cut continuous bias from 1/2 yard (.5 m) cotton and make 5/16" (8 mm) bias tubes, using the bias tube maker as an aid. Press tubes and cut in 5" (12.5 cm) lengths.

20.

Cut a strip of nylon seam finishing tape equal to the length of jacket front you want to edge with fringe.

21.

Center bias tubes, side by side, across seam finishing tape. Stitch down center of seam finishing tape to secure tubes. See Figure 9.

22.

Fold tape in half lengthwise; pin and baste to garment edge, as you would with piping.

23.

Pin jacket facing over basted tape, being sure to keep fringe free. Stitch and turn facing to inside. Press.

24.

Turn up hems, sew in shoulder pads, if used, and line jacket.

25.

Tie a single square knot in every second or third tube, to add fullness to the fringe.

TIPS

■ Short sewing machine stitches outline each colorful shape in this jacket, and the fashion fabric is cut away, leaving a raw edge that will fray a bit and give a "soft" finish. If you prefer a more polished look, cover the machine stitching with a satin stitch.

Exploring Expansion Vest

DESIGNER:

Katherine Tilton

THIS WILD AND WOOLLY MELTON VEST was inspired by traditional molas. The fabric is a perfect choice for appliqué techniques, because it doesn't ravel and comes in a dazzling array of colors.

MATERIALS

- Vest pattern of choice

- Felted wool melton in assorted colors, I yard (.95 m) total

- Wool jersey or double knit for binding

- One button to coordinate with design

TOOLS & SUPPLIES

- Scissors, rotary cutter

- Sewing machine

- Fabric paint of choice and ½" (1.25 cm) paintbrush

- Plain paper

- Pencil

INSTRUCTIONS

The vest will be constructed from pieced arrangements of melton, with additional appliqué shapes overlaid on top or reverse appliquéd underneath. The vest pattern, therefore, must be segmented into different color areas and shapes for the different fabrics.

1.

Preshrink all fabric.

2.

Cut jersey or double knit into 2" (5 cm) strips, for the armhole, neckline, and hem bindings. Hand paint design, as desired, and set aside.

3.

Make a full-size copy of the entire vest pattern onto plain paper that is sturdy enough to draw and erase on. Draw different pieced arrangements until you have a balance of shapes and sizes that you like.

4.

Starting with the largest shapes you have sketched, begin cutting out and pinning the design components together, following with the smaller shapes. (Alternatively, piece together a custom fabric and then lay out and cut the vest pattern.)

5.

When the design looks right, start sewing elements down. Remember that because the melton will not ravel, it can be sewn in lapped seams, rather than standard seams, and can be trimmed very close to the stitching. See illustration below. The lapped seam also reduces excess bulk, an important consideration for this heavyweight fabric.

6.

To add the overlay appliqué shapes, simply cut them out and edgestitch them to the right side of the vest.

7.

For the reverse appliqués, cut a piece of melton a bit larger than the design shape and baste or pin to the wrong side of the vest. On the right side, stitch the desired design and cut away the top layer of fabric close to the stitching, being careful not to pierce the layer below.

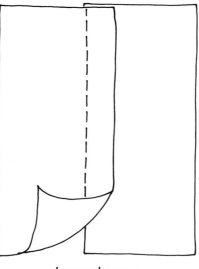

Lapped seam

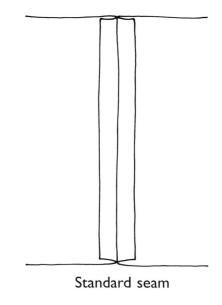

Standard seam

8.

When the body of the vest is completed, attach the knit binding. To do this, stitch strips together end-to-end, to make a continuous length of binding for the armhole openings and the front/neckline opening and hem. Stitch binding to right side of vest, trim seam, then turn binding to inside. To secure binding, hand sew to the inside or machine stitch in the well of the previous seam.

9.

In contrasting colors of choice, machine stitch design accents as desired on right side of vest.

10.

Attach button or other decorative embellishments, as desired.

TIPS

■ To felt the heavy wool melton coating fabric, the designer washes it in the hottest water possible, agitating it for about 30 minutes, and then drying it in the dryer.

■ If you have chosen a new vest pattern you haven't sewn before, make up a sample and fit it carefully before making the mola version.

■ Experimentation is the key to success when piecing shapes and colors together to make a custom fabric or garment. Play around with drawn or cut-out paper shapes before taking scissors to fabric, and be willing to continue experimenting right on through to the final steps of overlaying the appliqué shapes and the decorative machine stitching.

Jacket with Mola Panel

DESIGNER:

Lori Kerr

START WITH YOUR FAVORITE JAPANESE-STYLE TUNIC or asymmetrical-front jacket pattern, then customize the front panel to showcase an original mola design. Combined with multi-colored yarn couched to the surface, the mola appliqué is distinctive and stylish.

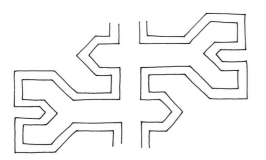

MATERIALS

- Tunic or jacket pattern with asymmetrical front
- Fabric for tunic/jacket pattern
- Assorted coordinating fabrics
- Variegated textured yarn of choice
- Variegated rayon machine embroidery thread
- Double-faced fusible stabilizer

TOOLS & SUPPLIES

- Pattern or tracing paper and pencil
- Chalk marker or disappearing ink fabric pen
- Sewing machine
- Iron

INSTRUCTIONS

1.

Trace the right front piece of the tunic or jacket pattern onto plain paper. Sketch ideas for couched yarn design and arrangement of appliqué shapes until you get an overall pattern you like.

2.

Iron stabilizer to wrong side of fabric selected for top layer of appliqué design. Transfer geometric pattern to stabilizer in a series of individual motifs or a continuous repeating line and cut out. You can also use parts of the pattern for separate appliqué shapes.

3.

Fuse geometric pattern to the background second layer. Thread sewing machine with selected rayon thread, and blanket-stitch around edges of the geometric mola design.

4.

Iron stabilizer to wrong side of background fabric. Trim the background layer to form a narrow outline or border around top layer.

5.

Cut right front piece out of tunic or jacket fabric.

6.

Peel the backing away from the two-layer geometric pattern and fuse it to the jacket front, according to your sketched design. Sew around all edges with machine blanket stitch.

7.

Repeat for other individual or continuous appliqué motifs.

8.

Using chalk or disappearing ink, mark the couched yarn pattern on the jacket front, following your sketched design.

9.

Zigzag over the textured yarn, using a thread that matches the tunic/jacket front and following the marked lines.

10.

Complete tunic/jacket assembly.

TIPS

- When considering sewing patterns for this type of design treatment, look for styles that have simple, straight lines. Stay away from darts, pleats, or other features that might interfere with the placement of appliqué shapes and couched yarn.

Ultrasuede Mola Coat

DESIGNER:

Mary S. Parker

MAKE A DRAMATIC ENTRANCE in this knockout of a colorful coat with mola design on the back.
Sewing the coat in Ultrasuede gives a depth and richness of color that won't fade.
Plus, it won't ravel, making it perfect for mock reverse appliqué.

MATERIALS

■ Piece of Ultrasuede large enough for the mola design's top layer, approximately 15 x 17" (38 x 43 cm)

■ Sturdy fabric for mola design's foundation layer, approximately 15 x 17" (38 x 43 cm); this can be Ultrasuede, also, but because it will be completely covered by the mola design, it can be another fabric type.

■ Assorted pieces of contrasting fabrics for inlay pieces of mola design

■ Coat pattern, fabrics, interfacing, lining, and notions of choice (coat shown here is made entirely of Ultrasuede)

■ Matching thread for coat and mola design

TOOLS AND SUPPLIES

■ Sharp scissors

■ Sewing machine

■ Universal point sewing machine needles. NOTE: Do not use leather needles on Ultrasuede.

INSTRUCTIONS

1.

Enlarge or reduce your own design or the mola design shown on page 120 to fit the upper back area of your coat pattern, omitting seam allowances and a small margin area to better "frame" your mola.

2.

Make a photocopy of the mola pattern and cut out of the paper all the areas that you will cut away from the top layer of Ultrasuede to expose the different color inlay pieces; this creates a pattern template you will use to cut the top layer of the mola.

3.

Pin the pattern template to Ultrasuede layer; place enough pins between the areas to be cut so the pattern will not shift as you are cutting.

4.

Following the pattern template, cut all the design shapes out of the Ultrasuede top layer and pin it to the foundation layer at the four corners.

5.

Starting from the center of the design, place a contrasting piece of inlay Ultrasuede in between the top and foundation layers, pin securely, and topstitch in place. Be sure that the inlaid piece is large enough to completely fill the space cut into the top layer. Trim the seam allowance of the inlaid piece close to the stitching, to reduce bulk, and reuse the trimmings as smaller inlay pieces elsewhere.

6.

Repeat with the other inlay pieces, working from the center to the outside edges and topstitching as you go.

7.

After you have stitched all the inlaid

pieces, topstitch the top and foundation layers around all four sides, about ¼" (6 mm) from the edge. Trim the foundation layer close to the stitching line, to reduce bulk and prevent its showing around the edges.

8.

Pin the mola panel to the back of the coat and sew in place with a fairly short zigzag stitch.

9.

Proceed with the coat construction, according to pattern instructions.

Tips

■ Ultrasuede will behave more like real suede if you "tame" it in the washing machine first. Wash and dry it at least half a dozen times, using heavy duty detergent and maximum agitation.

■ Ultrasuede is great for this mola project because it doesn't ravel, so you don't need to turn under the edges for the appliqué design. However, other types of non-raveling fabric, such as wool melton, will work also.

■ If your budget balks at the price of Ultrasuede, watch for special sales or offerings at your local fabric store. Some will have "scrap bags" of the material, sold by weight and at a fraction of the usual cost. These scraps are perfect for the small inlay pieces of the mola design.